high-vibrational *thinking*

how to
have great
relationships

steve wharton

foulsham
LONDON • NEW YORK • TORONTO • SYDNEY

foulsham

The Publishing House, Bennetts Close, Cippenham,
Slough, Berkshire, SL1 5AP, England

Foulsham books can be found in all good bookshops and
direct from www.foulsham.com

ISBN 0-572-03171-8

Copyright © 2005 Steve Wharton

Cover photograph by Image Source

A CIP record for this book is available from the British Library

Printed in Great Britain by Cox & Wyman Ltd, Reading, Berkshire

Contents

To Christina
Thank you. I love you.

Other books in the *High-vibrational Thinking* series:

HVT How to Beat the Blues 0-572-03177-7
HVT How to Feel Great About Yourself 0-572-03076-2
HVT How to Get Back to Work 0-572-03078-9
HVT How to Restore Your Life-Work Balance 0-572-03077-0
HVT How to Stop That Bully 0-572-03075-4

You Can Enjoy Great Relationships

I believe relationships provide us all with perfect challenges and opportunities for personal growth. In the midst of a relationship with a fellow human, we will push ourselves to the limits of endurance and so scale the heights of bliss and happiness. There is nothing like a relationship to teach us about ourselves; it is the perfect learning ground. Whether it is with our mother, father, husband, wife or indeed our children, this is where we make most progress in learning about ourselves.

Relationships are a wonderful gift, and each and every one of them should be cherished. There is no such thing as a wasted relationship because every one has something to teach us. You always come out of a relationship wiser than you went in, and the accumulation of wisdom is what life is all about. This helps us to help others, which in turn moves the human race forward in a positive way. You only have to look back a few hundred years to see how far we have come, and relationships, perhaps more than anything else, give us the wisdom to make our own invaluable contribution.

In this book I will concentrate on male and female relationships, taking an in-depth look at how they work in terms of this amazing world of energy that we live in. We will explore love in our relationships to discover how it really works– and also why sometimes it doesn't. We will look at the reasons why people grow apart– although I don't like to use the word 'fail'– why and relationships come to an end, as the time comes to move on. The most important thing to remember is that any relationship can be a wonderful experience and can offer marvellous opportunities for us all.

How this book works

The first section of this book explains what high-vibrational thinking is and how it works.

The second section shows you how to use high-vibrational thinking to understand what happens in your relationships. Using high-vibrational thinking– or HVT– will give you a much clearer picture of exactly what is taking place, as you look at the intricate workings of your relationships. You will be amazed at how simple things really are, as you begin to understand and see clearly why you and your partner behave as you do. With this new and very revealing way of looking at your life, you will have much more control over the negatives that can easily cause problems if left unattended. This newfound empowerment will lift your relationship to new heights and give you the necessary tools to enable you to stay there.

Our World of Energy

'If you want to find the secrets of the universe, think in terms of energy, frequency and vibration.' Dr Nikola Tesla, 1942

Dr Nikola Tesla was one of the foremost scientists of the early twentieth century. His outstanding intellect paved the way for a large number of modern technological developments; in fact, the tesla coil is still used in many television sets today. It is amazing to think that his words in 1942 should be still so relevant today. We now know that his understanding of the universe as energy, frequency and vibration was quite accurate. As we explore the intricate workings of the universe, unlocking the secrets of this amazing world of energy in which we live, this fact only becomes clearer.

Nothing you see around you is quite as it seems! The world that we live in is a huge ocean of energy, taking many different forms. The age of the microscope has shown us with abundant clarity that things that appear solid and static to us are in fact nothing of the sort. Even if the only science you know has been learnt from TV dramas about forensic scientists, you will be aware that if you look at an apparently solid object at a sufficiently powerful magnification, you will find that it is made up not from a single solid substance but from tiny particles vibrating at phenomenal speed. These tiny particles are known as neutrons, electrons and protons, and they link together to form atoms, the most basic building blocks of life.

What is perhaps even more astonishing is that atoms actually consist of 90 per cent empty space, which– by logical deduction– means that what we think of as solid, such as a concrete wall, is in fact mostly not solid at all! Nothing around us is actually solid, even though it may appear so; everything is made up of energy, vibrating constantly and at high frequency. This applies to everything you see around you: trees, houses, cars, walls, roads, dogs, cats, fish. It is a fundamental law of physics and applies even to us humans.

Each of these millions upon millions of different forms of energy vibrates at a specific frequency. The frequency at which it vibrates influences the form of the object. For example, the molecules of a solid vibrate very slowly; the molecules of a liquid vibrate more quickly; and the molecules of a gas vibrate even more quickly. Thus something with the same chemical composition can take different forms, depending on the vibrational frequency of its molecules. When the molecules are vibrating at their usual frequency rate, water appears as a liquid. Slow down that frequency and you get ice; speed up the frequency and you get steam.

We are all part of the energy exchange
As I have said, we are just as much a part of this cycle of energy as everything else around us. High-vibrational thinking (HVT) is based on that fact. Its fundamental principle is that we need to learn to see and think about our world in terms of energy.

High-vibrational thinking is a revolutionary new concept that taps into our knowledge of the movement of energy throughout the universe. It offers a way of seeing people– and the interactions between people– as part of a unique energy-transmission process that is hugely empowering to the individual. The first part of this book explains exactly how the system works. If you go back to fundamentals, it is really very easy to understand.

Just as ice, water and steam vibrate at different frequencies, so emotional energy also vibrates at different frequencies. As I will be explaining in detail later, positive emotions are high-vibrational energies, while negative emotions are low-vibrational energies. If we can find a way to maintain high-vibrational energy and deflect low-vibrational energy, then we can change our whole perspective on life. That's what HVT can help us to do. HVT is a system that takes positive thinking on to a whole new level.

HVT changes your perspective

This realisation throws a whole new light on how we perceive our world. Indeed, knowing how to use this information– and I'll be showing you that, too– can be hugely liberating and empowering, because it offers a way of using our knowledge to handle our lives in a more beneficial and productive way. This new perspective gives you far greater control over everyday situations and events you may previously have thought were largely beyond your control. With this knowledge comes power, and that power is the ability to choose more carefully how you relate to the energies that affect your life.

HVT will become automatic

What's more, once you have learned how to use this power, it will become an automatic way of thinking, and you can gain the benefits without even having to make a conscious choice about it. Once you have learnt to walk, you don't need to think about the process consciously any more. It's the same with HVT. Once you understand HVT, you will find that you automatically begin to incorporate it into your life as a working practice without any conscious effort on your part. Its positive influence on your life will be automatic, as the truth of HVT, once learned, cannot be ignored. Using HVT on a daily basis becomes a natural habit that will benefit every aspect of your life and help you to change in a positive and fulfilling way. All of a sudden, you will find that something inside you is monitoring the events and situations in your life and automatically responding to a negative situation in a way that will prevent it from dragging down the frequency of your energy field and making you feel bad.

A paradigm shift in consciousness occurs, and you find yourself able to deal with the negative events and situations that are part of everyday life in a new and positive way. HVT enables you to take control of events and situations rather than allowing them to control you. This is incredibly liberating, freeing your mind to direct your life in a much more productive and focused way.

Let's look at a simple example from one HVT course I have recently run. Within days of attending a course, two of my students found themselves turning off a particular television programme that they had been watching regularly for many years. They did not think about this action consciously until weeks later when it came up in conversation. Another student was talking about how negative this television programme had become. At that point, they both realised they had made the decision not to watch it any more immediately after attending the HVT course. Subconsciously they had sensed its negative impact and put a stop to it.

This kind of reaction is common among people who attend HVT courses, because they quickly learn to avoid engaging with damaging negative energies. You are already starting to learn that lesson simply by reading this book.

You too can learn automatically to handle situations and decisions in a more positive and beneficial way.

Essentially simple

The real strength of HVT is its simplicity and the fact that when applied to any subject it breaks down to a few basics. This enables anybody, whatever their age or background, to gain an understanding that previously may have seemed impossible. This is one of the reasons we have had so much success in working with children as young as 10 years old. Young people absorb the concept very quickly and find it easy to think in terms of HVT about every area of their life. It also means that the technique can be applied to any aspect of your life, regardless of your occupation or lifestyle. At school, it can give you more confidence and enthusiasm and help you to perform well. At work, it can cut negativity, create a better atmosphere and even increase productivity. In the home, it can reduce arguments and create a more loving environment.

Essentially, HVT is about making you feel good about yourself and maintaining that feel-good factor whatever life throws at you. Just think how much happier that could make you– not to mention the immeasurable stride forward in terms of moving our world into a brighter, high-vibrational future.

How Emotional Energy Vibrates

Now we understand that the whole world is part of a complex energy system, let's look specifically at how that affects us. Here, we are talking in terms of the power of emotional energy, and that is what we can harness to work to our advantage with HVT.

We have seen that– just like the objects around us– we are made up of energy and– like all forms of energy– our personal energy field vibrates constantly. The vibrational frequency of our energy field is affected by our thoughts and feelings. These are also made up of energy waves and influence our lives much more than we may realise. So depending on how we are feeling at any given time, the frequency at which our energy field vibrates can change dramatically.

Scientists and researchers in the USA have measured the frequency of the energy waves transmitted by the emotion of love, which they found vibrate very quickly, or at a very high frequency. Similarly, they measured the frequency of the energy waves transmitted by the emotion of fear, which they found vibrate very slowly, or at a low frequency. Our world exists within these two parameters.

Love is transmitted on a short wavelength, so it has a fast, high-vibrational frequency.

Fear is transmitted on a long wavelength, so it has a slow, low-vibrational frequency.

Think for a moment about listening to the radio, and this will help you to understand how it works. Radio stations are constantly transmitting radio waves. These are in the air all around us, even though we cannot actually see them. If your radio is not tuned into the right frequency, all you will hear is an annoying hiss. However, if you tune in your radio to the right frequency, you will be able to pick up on those radio waves so that you can hear and understand them perfectly, whether they are transmitting music, news, drama or comedy.

Happy is a high vibration
So whatever we are thinking and feeling has a very real effect, as it alters the frequency of our personal energy field. If we are happy, our energy is high-vibrational; if we are sad, our energy is low-vibrational. I am sure you are already getting the idea. Similarly, we can be affected by other people's thoughts and feelings. If you are unlucky enough to be in a room full of bored or unhappy people, it is very hard to remain upbeat and cheerful.

When we are full of laughter and joy, it makes us feel good. What is actually happening is that the high-vibrational energy of joy has pushed up the frequency of our personal energy field. We experience the same effect when we achieve something good, such as passing a driving test or an exam, scoring a goal, winning a competition or receiving praise for a job well done. What is happening here is the same: the achievement has suddenly made us feel successful and good about ourselves, again pushing up the frequency of our personal energy field.

So, as you can see, any thoughts and feelings that are positive– laughter, joy, honesty, sincerity, truth, compassion– are high-vibrational, keeping our energy field vibrating at the higher levels and therefore making us feel good. Just think about some of the expressions we use to describe that kind of feeling: 'I'm high as a kite', 'I'm buzzing', 'My mind's racing'. They clearly demonstrate that great feeling we get when we feel good, and they are referring to the frequency of our personal energy field. The faster our energy field vibrates, the better we feel, because that means we are closer to the frequency of love.

Of course, the opposite is also true. Anger, frustration, hate, jealousy, envy, greed and selfishness are all negative thoughts and feelings. Such emotions are low-vibrational; they slow down our energy field and make us feel bad. This is why we use phrases such as 'I'm down in the dumps' or 'I'm flat as a pancake'. The lower our energy field vibrates, the closer we are to the vibration of fear– which is not where we want to be!

Increasing our vibrational frequency

Even though this may be the first time you have thought about it in these terms, you probably will recognise that we spend most of our time trying to feel good about ourselves. In HVT terms, that means we are constantly seeking to increase our vibrational energy frequency.

There are a number of ways to try to do this– getting your hair done, buying a new car, having a drink, going out with friends, buying new clothes. They can all be effective, but if they don't affect your fundamental emotional state, the effect is not going to last very long. If you have ever got a buzz from buying a new pair of shoes, only to feel low again by the time you got home because you had nowhere to go to show them off, you'll know what I mean.

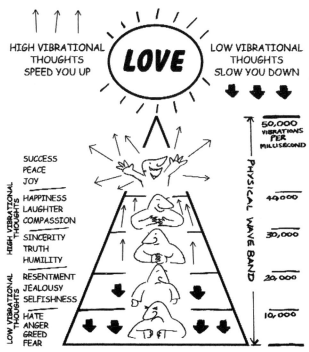

Hypothetically speaking, the physical waveband may run from 0 to 50,000 vibrations per millisecond. Our energy fields fluctuate between these parameters in our day-to-day lives. When we are happy and enjoying life, we may be vibrating at 35,000 vibrations per millisecond, but this may fall to 6,000 vibrations per millisecond when we are down in the dumps.

Some people take the search for a high to extremes, possibly drinking too much and experimenting with drugs. This may give a temporary 'high' but can very soon have the serious negative result of addiction.

That's where HVT comes in, because it is a way of educating ourselves so that our normal vibrational frequency is higher– plus it teaches us to control the effect of low-vibrational energy from other sources. It's just like exercising regularly to increase your resting heart rate. This not only makes you feel fitter, but it also makes it easier for you to cope with the physical demands of your everyday life.

How Our Emotional Frequency Is Established

As we spend most of our time trying to raise our vibrational frequency in order to feel better about ourselves, it makes sense to have a look at the factors that determine our individual energy level in the first place. This energy level is established and controlled primarily by our subconscious mind.

The conscious and subconscious mind

Your conscious mind is what you use to go about your everyday life– paying the bills, cleaning, sorting the washing, going to work. This is the methodical, reasoning part of your mind that carries out the daily tasks. It is the organised, sensible, logical part of you that understands how your world works. Your conscious mind automatically analyses any situation it confronts and plots the best and most logical way to deal with it.

Your subconscious mind, on the other hand, is a more complex entity, and is a source of immense power. It is affected by your surroundings in much more subtle ways and reacts most strongly to emotional stimuli.

Many psychologists refer to the subconscious mind as the 'inner child', because they feel that this best describes its characteristics. This terminology can help us to understand why our subconscious can sometimes pull us towards something that is not good for us. Imagine yourself as a child of five years old, with all the feelings and wonderment you had at that age; now imagine that this child is real and living inside you. Now you have a picture of your subconscious mind. It does not reflect you as you are now, with everything you have experienced and learnt over the course of a lifetime, but you as you were then. This child has no concept of what is good or bad for

Your inner child (your subconscious mind) will do everything it can to keep you in your comfort zone, even if this means holding you back in your life.

you; it just has its programming, which it will try to stick to regardless of what you may or may not consciously want.

In other words, we are all going through life trying to make some kind of progress but subject to the limitations that our subconscious mind places upon us. In terms of energy, our subconscious monitors us on a daily basis to keep us in what it has defined as our normal vibrational frequency zone.

Our formative years

The most important factor in determining this normal or average vibrational frequency level is the first five or six years of our lives. It is during these formative years that we establish our general thought patterns about ourselves. These first five or six years effectively programme our subconscious mind with certain beliefs about ourselves, which we then carry throughout the rest of our lives and which are very difficult to change. This vibrational frequency programming sets the boundaries for us and has a major bearing on every aspect of our lives from then on.

The most influential factors in our development are our immediate family and the environment we grow up in. In other words, the vibrational frequency of our environment and the frequency level of our family are what we pick up and become used to as our norm. When our mind is young and impressionable during those early years, we readily accept the situation in which we find ourselves. Because we don't know of any other situation, we unquestioningly believe that this is where we belong. This becomes the frequency zone we feel comfortable in and which, subconsciously, we spend virtually the rest of our lives trying to stay in.

So if you were brought up in a family with not much love (high-vibrational energy), you will believe that you only deserve a certain amount of love in your life, and your subconscious will use all its power to make sure that that is what happens. This will have massive repercussions, affecting your relationships, your work– in fact, everything you do in life. Your subconscious will stick to the programming, whether it's good for you or bad for you. In other words, it will monitor your vibrational frequency and keep it at the level that it is programmed to do.

As we grow up, our subconscious beliefs tend to become self-confirming because we constantly play them over in our subconscious mind, reaffirming our opinions and thoughts about ourselves. Most of the time, we are completely unaware that we are doing this. When we are constantly affirming to ourselves that we are not worthy (worthy meaning deserving of love, the highest-vibrational energy), we are keeping our vibrational frequency at the lower levels– and making life much harder for ourselves. The opposite is also true. If we constantly circulate high-vibrational thoughts about ourselves, we will keep our vibrational frequency at the higher levels, which in turn affirms that we are worthy and makes our life run much more smoothly.

Your inner child (subconscious mind) is much more in control of your life than you realise.

Of course, we have to acknowledge that we are all different and unique individuals with many varying factors determining our personality. This is why different people emerge from a similar upbringing with a different attitude to life. However, you are almost certainly reading this book because at least one aspect of your life can be improved, and understanding where any negative input may have come from is the first step towards being able to change the negative and maximise the positive.

The comfort zone

The energy level that we feel is where we belong is often referred to as our 'comfort zone'. We find it very difficult to break out of this zone, as our subconscious mind constantly draws us back to it as its starting point, regardless of whether it is in fact good for us or bad for us. This may seem strange but is in fact quite logical.

We tend to mix and feel more comfortable with people of a similar vibration rate.

You may, for example, feel uncomfortable in an upmarket, expensive restaurant, or perhaps you feel nervous when talking to professional people such as lawyers or consultants. What you are experiencing is a reaction to the frequency of the environment or person– if the frequency is vibrating at a higher rate than yours, you will probably feel slightly uncomfortable. This means you will seek out places and people with which you share a similar frequency, as this is where you naturally feel most comfortable.

Imagine carrying around with you an identity card that has not only all your personal details but also all your unconscious beliefs about yourself printed on it. If your normal vibrational frequency is low, your ID might list some of the following:

▸ You will only be shown a limited amount of affection from people who are close to you
▸ You are only allowed to have a low-paid job
▸ You are only allowed to live in a small house
▸ You are only allowed to have an old car
▸ You are only allowed to be average in what you do
▸ You are only allowed to wear casual clothes
▸ You will only be able to achieve a limited amount of success
▸ You will only ever have difficult relationships
▸ You will only ever have friends who take advantage of you

Now imagine that if you try to step out of line by going against these guidelines, you will be confronted by a police officer whose job it is to keep you within their confines. Let's say you manage to get a good job that pays well. Before you know it, the officer is on your case and starts talking you out of the job. You may find that you can't motivate yourself to raise your level of achievement as you need to in order to do the job well, so you start to make excuses and lay the blame elsewhere. Instead, you tell yourself that you work too hard or the firm is taking advantage of you, the pay is not adequate or you are not appreciated. This undermines your confidence and your ability to do the job well, and before very long you will find a way to give up the job while blaming everyone else.

I have seen this happen in my own experience. A very capable employee suddenly, after about three months in the job, begins to under perform. They start coming in late with any old feeble excuse, they cultivate an attitude of not been appreciated, they disrupt the other staff and in the end they push you so far that you have no choice but to let them go. When this happens, they insist that they are being victimised, they have done nothing wrong, and they may even threaten to take you to a tribunal. What they fail to acknowledge– even to themselves– is that it is their own behaviour that has caused the problem. The police officer has done his job and dragged them back into their low-vibrational comfort zone.

The problem with this situation is that we don't realise what is happening– that it is our own subconscious mind that is wreaking such havoc in our lives. It does not seem logical to believe that we would sabotage our own efforts, so we assume that the fault lies elsewhere.

I have experienced this myself, so I know how easily it can occur. When I was at school I was quite good at sport and soon found myself playing for the school teams. I did very well, and at one point it was expected that I might go on to a higher level. Once I realised that this was in prospect, I couldn't seem to motivate myself any more and decided to stop playing altogether. At the time, I just decided that I didn't feel like playing any more; it was only years later that I realised what had taken place. The threat of success had triggered off my subconscious programming, which dictated that I didn't deserve the high-frequency feelings that success could bring. These would have pushed me out of my comfort zone and into a new higher-frequency zone, so my subconscious mind convinced me that I didn't like sports any more and made me feel tired and unmotivated when faced with a game. Unfortunately for me, my subconscious won, and at 14 years of age I hung up my boots and, as a result, missed many years of enjoyment.

Not better but different

One thing always to remember, however, is that even if you start out with a low-vibrational energy field and feel uncomfortable with a different group of people, they are not 'better' than you. We all have our own qualities, strengths and weaknesses. You may want to be more like someone who has a high-vibrational energy field because they are fun to be around and are positive and more successful– that's fine. But that doesn't make them intrinsically better than you. Envy and self-criticism are both low-vibrational emotions, and if you give way to them, it will only make things worse.

You may, on the other hand, be someone who has had a good upbringing in a high-vibrational environment, leaving you with high-vibrational thought patterns. This gives you a much better chance of making the most of your life and better equips you to take advantage of opportunities that arise. You may still feel uncomfortable in places or with people where the energy pattern does not match your own– probably because your personal energy field is vibrating at a higher frequency– but it is important that you do not fall into the trap of believing that this makes you better in some way, for this is a damaging thought pattern. Arrogance and self-importance will pull down your energy frequency.

Don't try to place blame

It is important to point out here that your parents and their parents before them were also subject to this subconscious programming. However they brought you up, they were doing their best within their own programmed mental confines.

It is essential that you do not try to attach blame to anybody for your life as it stands at the moment. This would be to go straight down the low-vibrational route. Such thought processes are negative and low-frequency; they are certain to act as a dead weight around your neck and pull you down. Pointing the finger at others serves no purpose and will only harm you– by lowering your vibrational frequency. This is the time to assess the past and move on to the new, high-vibrational you.

How Our Emotional Frequency Affects Our Lives

The easiest way to demonstrate how limiting it can be to allow your subconscious mind to remain in control of your life is to take a look at a few examples.

Paul's comfort zone with crime

A few years ago, my work brought me into contact with a sales representative who proceeded to tell me a bit about himself. Let's call him Paul. Paul was brought up in a fairly tough environment, and his father had not been around much, as he had spent most of his time in prison for relatively minor offences. However, this childhood grounding had taken its toll, and, at 12 years old, Paul had found himself in trouble with the police for the first time for a minor crime. His family considered crime as a profession and accepted it as a normal way of life so, far from chastising him for having committed a crime, they were more concerned that he had not got away with it. This pathway continued. Paul's teenage years were littered with offences, but since he was behaving exactly according to his own idea of normality, he could see nothing unacceptable in this.

At the age of 25, during another stay in prison, Paul decided to go straight. He left prison with good intentions, found himself a job and at first managed to stay on the straight and narrow. It wasn't long, however, before he found himself drawn back to crime, even though he tried not to be tempted. When I spoke to him, he was very disappointed with himself and said that no matter how hard he tried, he kept finding himself committing offences. Although this made him feel bad about himself, when the temptation was there, he just could not resist it.

I wish I could tell you that this story has a happy ending, but I lost contact with Paul many years ago and do not know how his life has turned out. However, over the years, I have given Paul's story a great deal of thought. When I began to understand the workings of the subconscious mind, it became clear to me exactly what his problem was. Even though Paul wanted to stop being drawn to crime, his subconscious mind (inner child) did not. To his subconscious mind, crime was defined as normal behaviour– because this is what it had been programmed with during his first five or six years– and so was safely in his comfort zone. When, as an adult, Paul wanted to break out of his comfort zone, his subconscious mind took every opportunity to draw him back in.

When you think about how deep-rooted and fundamental our subconscious mind is to our entire personality, it is hardly surprising that it is very influential. We all have to contend with the daily tussle with our subconscious mind, but when we understand that it is simply trying to keep us within the boundaries of our own comfort zone, we have taken the first step towards doing something to take control over it.

Sue's comfort zone with food
Another friend of mine– let's call her Sue– has spent the last year or so trying to lose weight– something many of us have struggled with at some time. She has tried every

kind of diet, with the same results: she loses a few pounds at the beginning, but a few weeks later the weight is back on. Then it's on to the next diet regime. She has fallen into the trap of yo-yo dieting and is unable to maintain her ideal weight for any length of time. So why is it so difficult for Sue– like many of us– to get into new eating habits and stick to them?

Let's take a careful look at what is happening here. When Sue begins the diet, she really wants to lose weight and is fully motivated. She has the necessary willpower to control her eating habits. She knows that she will feel better and be healthier if she eats well and maintains the right weight for her height and build. The principles are easy enough to understand: eat the right amount of the right foods and she will lose weight. And with the range of healthy food options available these days, there is never even any need for her to feel hungry. Nevertheless, after the first few weeks, or even days, she finds herself drifting back into bad eating habits. Sue's favourite tactic is to move the goal posts. Having decided that she wanted to lose weight for an up-and-coming holiday, she then decides it's for her daughter's graduation ceremony, then for Christmas, then in the new year, and so on.

The problem is, of course, that Sue is obeying her inner child. Her subconscious is telling her that the unhealthy diet she has become used to or has cultivated over the years is what she should be eating. This kind of food is her comfort zone, and it is very difficult to leave it. 'No, you can't have any chocolate or sweets and you must eat plenty of fresh vegetables' isn't what Sue's inner child wants to hear. Sue's initial determination will control the child for a while, but very soon the child's persistence will be rewarded, because it just feels right to go back to your comfort zone.

Jim's comfort zone with keeping fit

Jim's story is another good example of how the subconscious mind sabotages our efforts to instigate change. When Jim first went to the gym he was filled with enthusiasm and energy for his get-fit project. Sure enough, the first few visits were easy, as he raced around the equipment, lifting weights, doing sit-ups and so on, quite possibly overdoing it in his eagerness to succeed. Then, after a while, the novelty wore off. Jim started to accept the feeblest excuses for not going to the gym– 'I have to take the dog for a walk', 'I feel a bit tired' and (an old favourite of many of us) 'I haven't got time'. Of course, just as Jim's initial determination had begun to wear off, his subconscious mind had kicked in, renewing its bid to regain control and pull Jim back into his comfort zone.

Your subconscious mind acts just like a child and soon gets bored.

Just imagine taking a five-year-old child to the gym with you. At first they may be excited and full of energy, dragging you around the gym and trying out all the equipment. This might continue for two or three visits, but then the child would begin to get bored and start whingeing about having to go. You would end up virtually dragging them there, and while you doggedly followed your keep-fit programme, the child would probably be sitting in the corner sulking.

This is exactly what happens in reality; only it's your inner child that behaves in this way. You don't realise that this is what is going on; you just feel the symptoms. Your enthusiasm wanes, you feel tired, you look for excuses not to go, and the next thing you know, you haven't been for weeks and you regret taking out a gym membership that commits you to the next– very expensive– six months.

Familiar story? I know it's happened to me on more than one occasion. Yet again, it's the subconscious mind dragging us back into our comfort zone– no wonder it is so hard to go forward in life when the most restricting factor is hidden in our own head. But remember, knowing what's going on is the first step towards being able to do something about it.

Jeff and Dave's stories
Another way to explore the notion of the comfort zone is to compare two people with similar upbringings. Jeff and Dave had known each other all their lives. They grew up together on a housing estate in a typical working-class environment. Their birthdays were only three days apart, and as children they were inseparable.

Jeff was the youngest of five children, with two brothers and two sisters. Life was quite hard for them, as their father and mother had separated when Jeff was only five years old, and during the time before the separation the house had been filled with arguments and anger as his parents struggled to cope. Jeff's father had never held down a job for long and spent most of his time drinking and gambling away the family's money on the horses. Money was therefore scarce, and Jeff had to rely on hand-me-down clothes from his older brothers. The family always had enough to eat, but there was no money for life's luxuries, such as holidays, treats or days out. All these factors combined to mean that the primary emotions surrounding Jeff in his formative years were anger, worry, self-pity, hostility, fear and a general sense of having less than everybody else.

As you will now recognise, all these emotions are low-vibrational. Naturally, they contributed hugely to how Jeff felt about himself. He felt that he wasn't as good as most of the other children because they seemed to have lots more than him, so his habitual thought patterns about himself were low-frequency: 'I don't deserve', 'I'm not as good as other people' and 'I can't do anything' were the kind of statements he would unconsciously repeat to himself. This negativity became Jeff's norm. His subconscious mind believed this was what he deserved to be, and it set about ensuring that this was what he got for the rest of his life.

Jeff was a very good soccer player and made the school team, but he found it hard to motivate himself and missed many chances of furthering his progress. He was quite bright but somehow could never be bothered to try hard enough, so he failed most of his exams. He could have made the swimming team but found an excuse so that he didn't have to take part.

When he left school, Jeff found work with an insurance company as a sales representative. He did okay, but somehow he was never going to be one of the high flyers. After a few years in this job he decided that selling insurance was too much like hard work and that he would do much better in a new job, even though some of the other reps were making good money and doing very well. He always had his own reasons for why they did better than him. It was because they had better areas than him or easier policies to sell. One thing was for sure: it was never his fault. So, Jeff continued moving from one job to the next over the next few years, not really getting on in any of them, because– according to Jeff– the other reps always had it better in some way. In the end, he put it down to the fact that he just didn't have any luck.

The crucial fact that Jeff wasn't aware of was that he himself was in control of his seeming lack of good fortune. His subconscious mind– programmed to believe that Jeff

Dave and Jeff had totally different outlooks on life: Dave was positive, Jeff was negative.

deserved to stay at a low frequency level– was monitoring his life all the way along. In order to keep him at his frequency level, it 'allowed' him only a very small amount of success– any more would have pushed him into a higher frequency zone. As soon as it looked as if he might become more successful, his subconscious mind kicked in and sabotaged any possibility of that happening. A little voice in Jeff's head would convince him that somebody had it in for him or he never got a fair chance or he should find another job because nobody in his current company appreciated him. This is how our subconscious mind keeps us within the comfort zone that it is programmed for.

Now let's take a look at Dave. Dave was an only child whose parents doted on him. His father was a foreman at the local steel works and his mother a very loving woman who spent her time looking after the family and their home. Dave's home was filled with love and positive energy. He remembers that his parents very rarely argued or had any kind of disagreement. Dave grew up a very happy child, whose parents gave him lots of attention and constantly told him that they loved him. Being an only child, he wanted for nothing. He always had fashionable clothes, and there were holidays abroad every year.

Growing up in this pleasant, loving, high-vibrational environment programmed Dave's subconscious mind to believe that this was the frequency zone in which he belonged. His habitual thought patterns about himself were positive: 'I know I can do it', 'I deserve the best', 'I am as good as anybody'.

Dave was never quite as good at soccer as Jeff, but he worked hard and with conviction, so he progressed further and made it to junior colts level with the local professional soccer club. Dave was not quite as bright as Jeff, but, again, he worked hard and eventually left school with good qualifications. After school, Dave followed Jeff into the insurance business and also became a sales representative. He always came in among the top two or three sales reps in the area. He loved his job, and his attitude impressed the management. He was soon promoted to area sales manager, then a few years later to regional sales director. Dave's life seemed charmed compared to Jeff's; everything always seemed to work out for him.

Jeff and Dave's friendship suffered over the years as their different life paths moved them into different social circles. Of course, they still spoke when they met, but after a while they found they had little in common, and their meetings became more of a passing hello than an in-depth conversation. In fact, Dave's success engendered not a little resentment in Jeff, which, sadly, estranged the two men even further.

Why our vibrational frequency is so important

Looking at Dave and Jeff's lives gives us an idea of how incredibly important our early years are in determining how easy the rest of our life is likely to be. Even though Dave was less talented and not as bright as Jeff, it was still much easier for him to be successful in life than it was for Jeff.

Dave's subconscious programming was of a much higher frequency than Jeff's. His feelings about himself and his own expectations were on a more high-vibrational frequency. He felt better about his abilities, so he had the confidence to try harder; he expected the best, so he impressed others with his positive attitude. All this enabled him to be successful at most of the things that he attempted. His subconscious mind monitored his life and kept him in the higher-frequency zone where it was programmed to believe he should be.

This meant that Dave saw life in a very different way from Jeff. What appeared to be insurmountable obstacles to

Dave had a much more high-frequency upbringing than Jeff, and this was the real difference between them.

Jeff were mere molehills to Dave. In a situation where Jeff's subconscious mind might say, 'That's just my luck; it will never work out for me', Dave's would say 'I'm always lucky; I know this will work for me'. Where Jeff's subconscious might say 'This job is a waste of time; everybody has an insurance policy', Dave's might say, 'I love this job; everybody needs insurance'. At higher frequency levels, life looks and feels completely different than it does at the lower levels. Jeff and Dave had exactly the same job, dealing with the same customers, and they had the same potential for success; the only difference was their vibrational frequency.

By now you will have a very clear idea of how our personal vibrational frequency can control our lives. You will soon begin to learn how high-vibrational thinking can help to change that frequency and put us back in control.

Frequency Variations

Before we move on to looking at how to start raising your vibrational frequency, there is one more issue to consider. That is how our average vibrational frequency changes naturally. Although it is true that the foundations of our subconscious, and therefore our average frequency level, are established at an early stage, our frequency level can and does change in relation to time, the people we interact with and the various challenges life presents us with.

We regularly encounter both high-vibrational and low-vibrational energy from both inside and outside. Here we are going to look at the energy we encounter from outside. How we cope with this on the inside is, of course, vital, so we'll look at this issue at the end of the chapter.

Frequency interaction
How we interact with other people has a major impact on our energy levels on a daily basis. In the case of Jeff and Dave in the previous chapter, we saw that Dave had a fundamentally positive, high-frequency energy, and because of this he made other people feel better too. The management recognised his potential, the customers were more responsive. This is because any interaction with another human being affects your frequency level. If you interact with somebody of a higher frequency, you will have your frequency pulled up; likewise, if you interact

with a person of a lower frequency, you will be dragged down. This is why some people feel very draining to be with, whereas others feel uplifting.

A positive, high-frequency attitude is great to be around.

It's easy to demonstrate this effect just by thinking about a few of the people you know. If you are having a conversation with someone who is enthusiastic, there's lots of high-vibrational energy around. You can chat for hours without the conversation lagging. On the other hand, if you are having a conversation with someone who is unhappy, there's so much low-vibrational energy that you may struggle to keep the conversation going. You are being affected by this person's low-vibrational energies– as they are likewise affected by your vibrational frequency.

Similarly, if you are yourself feeling down while you are trying to cheer someone else up, it will be much harder work. In fact, it's quite likely that you will both ending up crying into your beer! On the other hand, if you are feeling pretty good at the start of the conversation, they may pull you down a bit, but it is more likely that you will be able to raise their spirits and help them to feel better.

The more you can be around high-vibrational energy, the more it will benefit your own energy levels on a daily basis. And if you are constantly around high-vibrational people, then the impact can help to stimulate a long-term improvement in your own energies. You really are fundamentally affected by the company you keep.

Places also have a vibrational frequency to which we react. We all have places that we love and others that we find intimidating or uncomfortable. Some towns feel depressing and unwelcoming, whereas other towns feel upbeat and pleasant. Here, we are simply picking up on the collective vibrational frequency of the people who live there.

Changing energy frequency levels

As we progress through our lives, we may find that we achieve success in different things– perhaps our career takes off and we become very good at what we do. This increases and reinforces our good opinion of ourselves, giving us more confidence in our own ability and changing our personal thought patterns. This means that our personal energy frequency rises. A similar, negative, effect can occur if you have a run of bad luck. If you find the problems you encounter too much to cope with, they are likely to depress your vibrational level.

We all experience natural vibrational fluctuations on a daily basis as we encounter and have to cope with life's everyday events. We have probably all experienced the feeling of being down in the dumps, when our problems seem huge and we can't see a way around them. If we have an interrupted night's sleep and wake up on a rainy day to news of a traffic jam on our route to work on the local radio, it can make things feel even worse. But with a good night's sleep and a ray of sunshine when you open the curtains, you feel a new surge of energy and yesterday's problems diminish. What is happening is we are viewing the same situation from a different frequency level.

Anna's typical day

Let us imagine that during any given day we have 100,000 thoughts going through our mind. These thoughts are influenced by day-to-day activities– people we meet, situations we encounter, whether our favourite team wins or loses, news in the newspapers and so on. The thoughts we have may be high-vibrational or low-vibrational, and each one has an influence on the vibration rate of our personal energy field, speeding it up or slowing it down as we go about our daily activities. Let us take a look at a typical day to give you an idea of how it works.

8.00 a.m.

It's a bright spring morning, the sun is shining, and as Anna throws back the curtains, the sun's rays cascade into the bedroom. The children are relaxed and happy as they get ready for school. Anna's thoughts are **high-vibrational**, she feels content and her personal energy field is vibrating at a fairly fast rate.

8.30 a.m.

This is a great start, but little Lucy is lagging behind. 'Come on, Lucy. Hurry up or you will be late for school,' shouts Anna, feeling frustrated. This is a **low-vibrational** emotion, and it slows down Anna's personal energy field.

9.00 a.m.

'But it's still a great day,' Anna thinks to herself as she sets off for school. A few jokes on the way ensure a happy and laughter-filled journey so, as this is a **high-vibrational** situation, it speeds up her personal energy field.

9.30 a.m.

The children are safely in school when up strolls Mrs Johnson. 'Oh, no!' Anna says to herself, 'who is she going to be gossiping about today?' Anna's personal energy field slows down as she lends a sympathetic ear to Mrs Johnson's jealousy, resentment and envy. The **low-vibrational** conversation drags down Anna's energy field.

Anna's vibrational level is lowered by contact with another person's negative energy.

10.00 a.m.

The journey home is uneventful; a good thing really, because Anna is now in no mood for any aggravating drivers. At home, the post is waiting.

First, the gas bill: it's slightly more than she was expecting; can their budget can cope with it? **Low-vibrational** thoughts creep in, slowing down her energy field.

Next, the electricity bill. That's a lot lower than she expected, and a small wave of **high-vibrational** joy sweeps in. Up goes her personal energy field.

Next, the credit card statement: not so bad!

But then she opens the telephone bill: £500! A flood of **low-vibrational** emotions hit: worry, fear, anger. Anna's personal energy field plummets as she engages in this **low-vibrational** energy. Now she has a headache as well.

11.00 a.m.

Anna spends the rest of the morning fretting over her financial problems and feeling very low indeed. Suddenly her **low-vibrational** state is interrupted by the doorbell. As she opens the door, Anna is greeted by a big smile from Jane, her next door neighbour. 'Put the kettle on,' says Jane as she charges by, brimming with confidence and **high-vibrational** energy. After an hour's conversation, Anna feels decidedly better. Jane's high-vibrational attitude has put her problems in perspective, and Anna's personal energy field has shot up. Jane dashes off to her mother's, and Anna decides it's time to do the shopping.

12.00 noon

The sun is bright (although Anna had failed to notice it during her **low-vibrational** morning). Her first stop is the butchers, who is always very friendly. A well-placed compliment pushes up the frequency of her personal energy field.

Anna's vibrational level is raised by contact with another person's positive energy.

12.30 p.m.

Soon the shopping is done, and Anna heads back to the car park, laden down with bags. As she approaches the car, a car hurtles by at speed. It narrowly misses her, but she drops one of her bags of shopping– eggs, tins and fruit fall everywhere. Her initial feelings are fear and panic, but they are soon followed by frustration and anger. She decides to report the incident to the police. By this time her personal energy field has plummeted as a result of all this **low-vibrational** energy.

Anna's vibrational level plummets as a result of stress and anger.

2.30 p.m.

After two hours in the police station, Anna is feeling very fed up. The possibility of anything being done about the incident appears to be nil. Anna trudges out. Her personal energy field is now very slow indeed. To compound the situation, she is running late to pick up the children, who immediately sense Anna's bad mood. Once in the house, she chases them upstairs to do their homework while she makes the tea, her mind racing with the day's events and focusing on **low-vibrational** thoughts. Her personal energy field is slowing down even further and her mind is pulsating with anger, which she is ready to direct at her husband when he gets home.

*Anna prepares to direct her low-vibrational mood
towards her husband.*

5.00 p.m.

'Hello, darling!' shouts John, as he opens the front door.
Anna is ready for him, fired up and angry, but he stops her
dead in her tracks. 'For you,' he says, handing her a dozen
red roses. 'I've booked a table at our favourite restaurant to
celebrate my promotion! All of a sudden Anna's anger and
fear vanish and her personal energy field races up. 'It was
nothing really,' she blurts out. 'Anyway, let's celebrate!
What marvellous news!' The children sense that the
atmosphere has changed from **low-vibrational** to **high-vibrational** energy.

7.00 p.m.

A short while later, as she lies soaking in a hot bubble bath
with a wonderful night in front of her, Anna thinks back
over her day and begins to recognise how she became the
victim of her own thinking. Every time she allowed a
thought to grab hold of her and control her without
offering any resistance, she became the victim of all the
low-vibrational energy that had come her way. But, she
realises, she did not have to engage with these **low-vibrational** energies quite so eagerly. If she could have

detached herself from them, her personal energy field would not have been quite so affected.

Anna's energy field

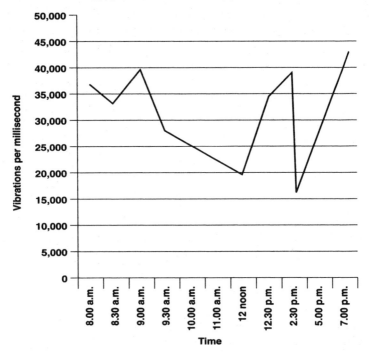

Fluctuations in Anna's energy field throughout the day.

As you can see from the graph, Anna's personal energy field has fluctuated throughout the day as she alternated between positive and negative thoughts– from a low point of 17,000 vibrations per millisecond at 2.30 p.m., when she had just left the police station, to a high point of 48,000 vibrations per millisecond at 7 p.m., as she lay in a hot bath with only positive thoughts in her mind. Remember, the faster our personal energy field vibrates, the better we feel, because we are closer to the high-vibrational energy of love.

Coping with negative energy

It doesn't matter what is pulling you down– the gas bill, the TV breaking down, the children stressing you out. You cannot avoid the low-vibrational energy in your environment; this is the very nature of life. What does matter is how you choose to react to these low-frequency attacks, because you can have some control over how much these situations and events affect you.

I recall an incident in my office in which one of the administrators had had a particularly stressful morning dealing with complaints of various sorts. This low-frequency energy had given her a headache. Then the telephone rang and she found out that she had just won quite a large amount of money. She happily passed on the story of her good fortune to the rest of the staff. A little later, I asked her if she still had a headache. To her amazement, she replied that it had completely disappeared. You see, sometimes even headaches can be instantly cured if you can find a way to lift your personal energy vibration.

On another occasion, a boy I know called Jordan lost his brand-new mobile phone. He was distraught, as his father had just bought him this expensive present. When he realised that he had lost his phone, his whole day looked completely different: one minute he was happy and enjoying himself and the next he was inconsolable. His mind had suddenly become filled with low-vibrational emotions: worry, fear, anger, frustration, disappointment. This had the effect of pulling down his energy frequency. It was several days before Jordan recovered and moved back up to his normal frequency level. That's how powerful negative energy can be.

If negative energy is so powerful, you need an equally powerful weapon to use against it– and that's high-vibrational thinking.

Taking Control

So let's briefly recap. Energy is vibrating all around us. The energy of love is high-vibrational; the energy of fear is low-vibrational. The closer we can stay to the vibration that we call love, the better we will succeed in all aspects of our lives.

Most of life's problems exist at the lower frequency levels, so if you are focused on low-vibrational energy, you are likely to be ill more often, end up in more arguments, have more trouble with your car or your computer, find it harder to get a job or succeed at work, and experience problems at school or with the children. In fact, everything will be much more difficult.

High-vibrational thinking is a way of learning to dismiss low-vibrational thoughts and replace them with high-vibrational thoughts. It makes absolute sense to try to think in a more high-vibrational way, because this puts you in control. And being able to control your thoughts and feelings will help you to change your life. You can learn to use high-vibrational thinking in every aspect of your life. You deserve the positive energies of love, happiness and joy in your life just as much as anyone else.

Just being aware of high-vibrational thinking is the first step to taking control of your energy field, as it enables you to understand what is happening in your mind and to appreciate that control is lacking. Once you have taken that first step, it won't be long before you automatically begin to assess situations in terms of energy and put HVT into practice without thinking about it. This makes a welcome change from being controlled by negative energies, tossed around like a rag doll in the wind.

Reprogramming our subconscious

There are two elements in making HVT work for you: one deals with your fundamental energy levels, and the other deals with how you react to the changing energy levels around you.

The influences we experience during our formative years help to establish our normal vibrational frequency and define our comfort zone: our fundamental feelings about ourselves and the kind of life we believe we deserve. Throughout our life, our subconscious mind monitors our feelings and actions so that we stay within the boundaries of our comfort zone– whether that is good for us or not. If we try to move away from that comfort zone, we are engaging in a battle for control– and it's a battle that we usually lose.

There is another way– one that avoids the battle and enables us to take control. The answer is to re-programme your subconscious mind and so change the boundaries of your comfort zone.

Let's take the dieting example that we looked at on pages 27–8. While your comfort zone is chips, chips and more chips, any diet will be a huge struggle that is almost doomed to failure, because you will be constantly drawn back to your comfort zone. But if you change the boundaries of your comfort zone, your subconscious mind will monitor what you eat to keep you at the newly programmed weight that is now within your comfort zone. You will be able to change your eating habits, with the result that you are attracted to a more healthy diet of less fattening foods. If you look at those people who have dieted successfully and lost lots of weight permanently, you will generally find that they have also managed to reprogramme their subconscious mind successfully.

If it's improved fitness you are trying to achieve, the principles are just the same. While your comfort zone is an evening with your feet up in front of the TV, that is what your subconscious will be pulling you towards.

HVT is a way of reprogramming that does away with the need for an iron will. This book will show you how to achieve that reprogramming. The first step towards change is to understand how your mind works and accept the power of the subconscious mind. Once you appreciate this, you can begin to move forward and make plans for a new and exciting future.

With HVT you can retrain your inner child.

Of course, once you have reprogrammed your subconscious into a new comfort zone, it will start to form new and more positive habits. If you have an established habit of taking regular exercise, when you miss your exercise for some reason, you will feel tired and drained. It's almost as if you are addicted to exercise and without it you feel down. This, again, is your subconscious pushing you to stick to the comfort zone– but in this case, of course, the comfort zone is healthy, so the subconscious is a force for good.

So you can see that your subconscious can be programmed for success or failure, and it will use all its powerful influence to maintain whatever it is programmed for. If we can reprogramme our subconscious for success, clearly this is the answer to many of our problems. This book will show you how to do just that– to change your subconscious comfort zone in relation to the specific problems and issues that are relevant to you.

Start changing now

You don't have to wait until you have read the whole book to make changes in your life. You can start making changes straightaway. Start by dealing with the energy fluctuations you encounter on a daily basis and how you react to them.

Remember the outline of Anna's fairly ordinary day (see pages 39–44). Look at it again and you will see how Anna allowed herself to be engaged by the energies around her rather than taking control of her own energy field. When she encountered low-vibrational energy from outside, or when her own emotions were low-vibrational– both things we can't always avoid– she allowed herself to be dragged down and ended up feeling even worse. You are probably just the same. Now that you realise that by engaging with low-vibrational thoughts you are only going to damage yourself by dragging down your personal energy field, you can start to implement changes that will make an immediate difference to your life.

Don't engage with low-vibrational energy

The crucial thing is not to engage emotionally with low-vibrational energy, because it is when you become emotionally attached to negativity that you are most damaged. Your personal energy frequency will plummet and move you into a much more difficult frequency zone.

You can now recognise low-vibrational energy as anything that pulls you down and makes you feel negative: anger, disappointment, envy, spite and so on. When you encounter that kind of energy, the secret is to remain calm and to let the negative energy pass over you without buying into it. Try to visualise the energy moving away from you and disappearing, rather than hanging on to it and engaging with it mentally. The principle is very simple: recognise it and reject it.

Start right now. The next time you find low-vibrational thoughts coming into your mind, let them go. You almost certainly won't succeed straightaway; it will take a little practice, but even the first time you try it, you will feel some impact. Then, every time you succeed, it will become easier and more automatic to reject negativity. If you stick at it and follow the specific guidance in this book, you will get better at it every day.

Take bills as an example. If you have a gas bill that is higher than you expected, you obviously have to do something about it. But worrying is not going to make the bill any smaller; nor is it going to get it paid. If you put aside the worry, you have more energy to think about positive things that will help you to solve the actual problem of paying the bill. Your mind will be able to focus on the options: you can dip into your savings, contact the supplier and arrange to pay it off gradually, turn down the heating thermostat so it doesn't happen again– or whatever.

Concentrate on the present

So visualising negative energy draining away will help. Another very simple way to handle low-vibrational thought patterns is to concentrate on the present.

We all spend too much of our time thinking about the past or the future. Our minds tend to dwell on something that has happened or something that might happen until this becomes a habit that is difficult to break. In fact, we are often scarcely aware that we are doing this.

It is all too easy to dwell on a low-vibrational event that has happened in the past: the time we struggled to meet a payment date; the time someone shouted at us or let us down. We keep running it over and over again in our minds like some kind of loop-tape action replay. The result of replaying thoughts of anger, frustration, disappointment, fear or uncertainty is that our personal frequency level is dragged down even more, pulling us down into a negative zone.

Likewise, we may focus our attention on a future negative event that may never happen: the cold we are sure we are going to catch, the redundancy that is bound to come, and so on. Similarly, the effect is to lower our frequency level, leeching away all our positive energy.

The past is gone and we cannot change it. Dwelling on its negative energies will only drag us down. We simply need to learn from it and move on. The future is not here yet; worrying about something that may or may not happen will only drag down your personal energy field, making life much harder in the process.

If you can avoid this time trap and think in the present, you will find that your energy levels remain high. By being alert to this pitfall, you can train your mind to recognise when you are about to fall into the trap. Then you simply stop and remind yourself to concentrate on the present. If you have a problem, look at what you can do now to solve it in the best possible way.

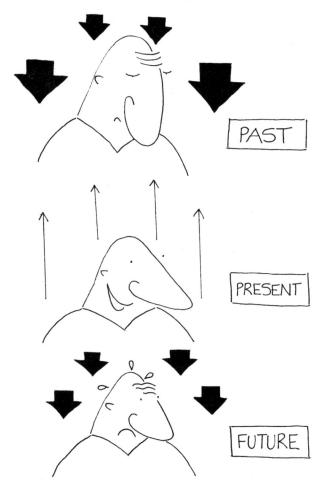

Dwelling on the past and worrying about the future is a waste of energy. Stay focused in the present if you want to get the best out of your life.

Use high-vibrational thinking to clear your mind of clutter and stay focused in the present moment; then you are ready to handle life to the best of your ability.

Take one step at a time

There will be times when you don't manage to dismiss low-vibrational thoughts altogether. Don't worry about it– for worrying is in itself hanging on to low-vibrational energies. Look at what you did achieve; tell yourself how much better you did it than last time; congratulate yourself and move on. Before long you will find that you are more and more in control. This means that your personal energy field will not slow down as easily next time you encounter low-vibrational energy, and you won't have to spend every day on a mental rollercoaster ride.

Remember, you are more in control than you realise. Your thoughts create your reality, so if you fill your mind with high-vibrational thoughts, you will have a more positive, enjoyable and fulfilling life. You can take control of your own energy.

What Is Love?

We already know love is a form of energy and is the fastest-vibrating energy that we know. To feel this energy we have to find a way to raise our own personal energy vibration rate, so that we resonate at the same speed as the energy that we call love. If we can achieve this, then we can feel all its amazing power and this is the most wonderful feeling imaginable. Even just speeding up our personal energy field a little will enable us to feel better, as the closer we can get to the vibration of love the more of it we can feel. This is why we spend most of our lives trying to make ourselves feel better; we are simply longing to raise our energy frequency. The most powerful catalyst available to achieve that is to connect up with another person in a positive, intimate relationship. There is nothing else like it to give us the boost that we all unconsciously crave; it's the very driving essence of our soul, to resonate at the same vibration as the energy that we call love.

So from this we can see that love is a state of being and something that you must attain, somebody else can direct love (high-vibrational energy) towards you and this is a wonderful feeling, but real long-lasting love must come from within. So when another person 'loves you', this means that they care very deeply about you, only wishing you good and generally only directing positive thoughts towards you. They in effect have high-vibrational thoughts about you and this makes you feel better about yourself, giving a boost to your personal energy vibration rate. To be truly 'in love' you have to align your personal energy field to the same vibration rate as the energy of love. This means that real love comes from within and not from outside of you, as when you vibrate at the same frequency as love, your entire being fills up with this blissful energy and you can feel it brimming over and pouring out of you.

Amazing experience

A number of years ago I had an amazing experience. I was going through a particularly stressful period and remember feeling very down and desperately searching for an answer to my problems (just the usual problems that we all encounter, of course, which can sometimes seem huge and insurmountable). I found it difficult to sleep and remember mulling things over and over in my mind, until eventually I fell into a deep sleep. The next thing I knew, the sun was shining through the blinds and I could hear the birds singing. For some completely inexplicable reason I felt absolutely great and on top of the world; the huge problems that had so engulfed me the previous evening now seemed trivial. I had never felt better in my life and I set off to work in an almost dream-like state as the world had taken on a whole new and exciting persona. Everything looked different to me, the grass was greener than I had ever noticed it before, and the sky was an incredible blue, somehow brighter and deeper than I had ever seen it.

When I got to work, the amazement continued. Everyone I met appeared to have bright shining eyes, as if some kind of energy was pouring out from deep within them. Their faces were shining with joy and they all looked so beautiful. I remember feeling such compassion and love for everybody, it was almost like I wanted to take care of everybody and look after them. This incredible feeling lasted for about one month and it is an experience that I will never forget. I was so disappointed as my old feelings slowly reappeared and desperately tried to cling on to this amazing and beautiful feeling of unconditional love that I had inexplicably come across.

At the time I never fully understood what had actually taken place. I just knew something profound had happened to me. It was almost impossible to explain my experience to other people, as my lack of real understanding made it difficult to put it into words. It wasn't until some years later, as my understanding of high-vibrational thinking grew, that I actually appreciated what had really taken place. Somehow, for one month I had come close to resonating at the same frequency as the energy we call love. I don't know why this happened to me, I just know that it did. This incredible experience then became my life's goal; I wanted to get that feeling back and it was high-vibrational thinking that gave me the understanding of how to achieve that.

The ultimate goal

My feelings now about that amazing month of my life are that I had experienced what it must feel like to enter into the state of being that we call love, or as some teachers describe it, to attain enlightenment. This, of course, is the ultimate goal of many a seeker of wisdom and happiness, and you will find reference to this in many books and teachings. My personal view of enlightenment now is that to attain enlightenment you must reach a state of being where you have no low-vibrational thoughts or feelings in your mind. You are so free of negativity that your personal energy field rises and you bask in the frequency of love.

As I look back on that time, I feel I have now come to a clear understanding of what actually happened. The stress and pressure that I felt at that time had somehow triggered off a reaction in my mind that had made me let go of all of the low-vibrational thoughts and feelings I was carrying and allowed my personal energy frequency to rise. The feeling was indescribably beautiful and on reflection I now realise that this is what we are all really seeking. The only thing holding us back from this is the low-vibrational thoughts and feelings that we constantly carry in our minds. It's simple: take all of the low-frequency thoughts and feelings out of your mind and your personal energy frequency will rise, moving you closer to the frequency of love.

Unconditional love
Unconditional love is what we feel for our children. No matter what they do we still love them; we don't lay down stipulations that they have to abide by to receive our love. In other words, as we now understand that love is actually an energy and that to be in love is a state of being, then the unconditional love that we have for our children means we care very deeply about them and want the best for them. We have for them the most pure and positive thoughts, and the feeling of love that wells up inside of us for them is a very high-vibrational energy, void of negativity. This beautiful feeling is totally sincere and gives us a glimpse of what we are capable of feeling for everybody, including ourselves.

The first and most important step towards achieving this is to learn to love ourselves, as this is the main source of the negative thought patterns that plague our lives. If we can wipe away the pain that our subconscious mind (inner child) is carrying, we could be well on the way to the higher vibrational levels. As we looked at earlier in the lives of Jeff and Dave (see page 30), the pain that we carry has generally been put in place during our first five or six years and acts as a dead weight as we go through the rest of our lives. This pain lodged in our subconscious mind has a massive influence in every area of our life and very often it is a hurdle that we never overcome. It is like a big heavy bucket of negativity and as long as we hold on to it we can never rise up and fully experience the beauty of love. To achieve your potential and rise up the frequency scale you must let go of the bucket and stop allowing it to hold you down.

Conditional love

In a romantic relationship, this can be totally different; we can be totally in love with somebody but this love is often subject to certain conditions. As long as the person receiving our love behaves as we want them to, then we will continue to love them; but if things change, then we begin to withdraw our love from them. This is conditional love and what we are really saying when we behave in this way is, as long as you make me feel better about myself then I will love you, but the moment that you stop making me feel better about myself, then I will stop. You are in effect using them to give your vibration rate a boost, and as soon as they stop doing this you retaliate by withdrawing your positive energy from them. This means you are happy as long as they say nice things about you, look up to you, admire you, depend upon you, need you. You are using them to feel better about yourself, because if you really loved them you wouldn't care whether they did this or not. Just like your children you would love them regardless. This conditional love is always destined to failure, as sooner or later they will let you down and your automatic reaction will be to withdraw your affection. This is why most relationships start off on a blissful high as you both enjoy the rise in vibration that you give each other. This is sometimes referred to as the honeymoon period, but unfortunately this usually doesn't last, and before long you are falling down the vibrational scale, falling out of love.

The three zones of relationships

The first thing that you need to do is look at this in terms of HVT, which means understanding what is taking place in respect of energy.

What has energy got to do with relationships you may wonder? In fact, that is exactly what every relationship is: a coming together of energies. The two energy fields, male and female, connect in a very intimate and personal way. This connection runs deep on a mental and physical level, which results in two people gradually having more and more influence on each other.

When two people start a relationship

If you can imagine what happens when two people first start going out with each other, the very act of one person finding another person attractive is complimentary. Asking somebody out on a date and being accepted is a very positive situation. The person being asked out feels elated because somebody actually finds them attractive. This makes them feel good about themselves, which in turn boosts their vibration rate. This very positive statement— that they are deserving of love (high-vibrational energy)— lifts their opinion of themselves. The other person also gets a huge boost in vibration because to be accepted is also a very positive experience. It helps to drown out any low-vibrational thought patterns and gives them a lift up the frequency scale. All of a sudden you both forget all your everyday problems and feel on top of the world, as you bask in the higher vibrational levels. You are in love.

Well that's what we call it. What has actually happened is the positive attention that we are giving each other has pushed up our personal energy frequencies, moving us both closer to the frequency of love. This enables us to feel the beautiful blissful power of love and all we want to do is stay there. The feeling is wonderful and all of a sudden life appears to be totally different.

All the positive implications of a new relationship propel our energy upwards. Very little negativity is present in the early part of a relationship, as the good feelings far outweigh the bad. It seems that we are virtually on a constant high, as the attention from our new partner boosts our confidence. The message echoing through our

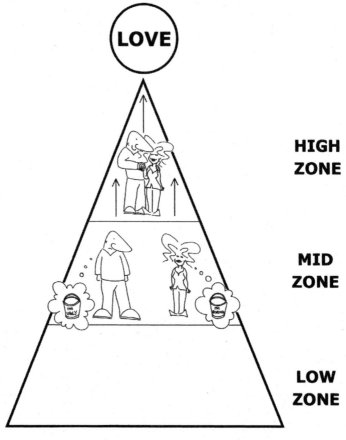

When two people first fall in love, they forget their usual negative thought patterns for a while and rise up in vibration.

subconscious mind is that somebody loves us and we enjoy the good feelings that this brings with it. Our belief in our self worth soars, as for a time we forget our usual low-vibrational thought patterns about ourselves and the world around us. The negativity that so often pervades our thoughts is temporarily suspended and replaced by a newfound belief in ourselves, which is a by-product of our new situation. Suddenly life seems wonderful and exciting, as we float in the beautiful feelings evoked by meeting this new person and falling in love with them. It really is an amazing experience and one that we all crave, because to rise up the vibrational scale gives us a much more positive opinion of ourselves. This is what life is all about and there is nothing like falling in love to give us this boost in frequency. Many other things might make us feel better, but they really do pale into insignificance compared to falling in love. This is the real natural high of life and anything else is just second best.

Relationship zones

I see relationships falling into one of three separate zones: high, mid and low. These zones are defined by the vibrational frequency of the relationship, high being the highest and so on. Let's take a detailed look at what the main differences are in the three zones.

High zone

When you first fall in love with somebody you rise up to the high zone, because your personal energy vibration is closer to the vibration of love. This is the honeymoon period when you are deeply in love and everything seems so wonderful. This is where you are both very positive to each other and negativity is, for a while at least, in a fairly dormant state.

Mid zone

When the vibration of your relationship starts to fall you
enter the mid zone, where of course you still love your
partner, but that magic sparkle seems to have diminished
somewhat. As you have become used to each other, the
beautiful exciting feeling of the high zone has dwindled

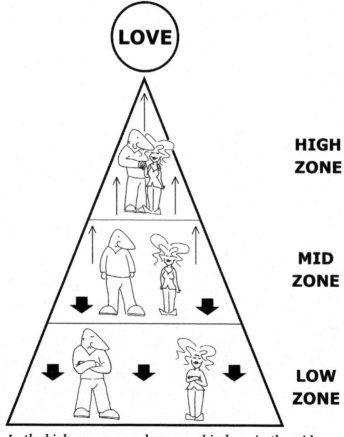

*In the high zone we are happy and in love; in the mid zone
we are back to 'normal'; in the low zone we find our
relationship a struggle.*

away. This is where you can spend many happy years with your partner and be satisfied and content, even though the magic has subsided. This is the zone where most long-term relationships find themselves settling and many entire lifetimes are spent here.

Low zone

Relationships can prove to be very difficult in the low zone, as you are now dropping well away from the vibration of love. This can be a very dysfunctional place to find yourself, and low self-esteem and abuse are prevalent here. Many relationships in this zone have little chance of survival. People that do stay together in this zone are often dependent on each other, due to massive personal insecurities. They can be so scared of being by themselves that they prefer to remain in a very negative relationship than actually face life alone. This can result in years of misery and unhappiness chained into an emotional prison of their own making. Bullying is commonplace here– and even physical violence.

In general

The mid zone in relationship terms is where most of us are, and the high end of this zone is not too bad a place to be. The further down the mid zone you slide, the further away from love you are getting, so the worse it feels. Many couples find themselves tied into mid zone relationships due to responsibilities and accept this as perfectly normal. Remember: relationships teach us a lot about ourselves, and the lower our relationship in vibrational terms the more opportunities we are going to have to learn.

What Happens When We Fall Out of Love?

Falling out of love means that you are falling down the vibrational scale away from the frequency at which love vibrates. The further you fall, the less love you feel. You must keep your energy frequency vibrating at the higher levels to stay in love.

The reason that we fall out of love when we are gaining our rise in vibration from somebody else and not from ourselves is that it is inevitable that, sooner or later, they will do something that will contravene our idea of how they should behave. This is the very nature of life on our planet and in 99 per cent of cases unavoidable, as we live in a world full of low-vibrational energy. Of course, we must also accept our own responsibilities when this arises, as it is equally difficult for our partner to maintain their love for us when we, too, are subject to the continual ups and downs of life. To stay in love you must learn how to handle low-vibrational energy, so that when you come across it as little damage as possible is done. This can be achieved through the use of HVT in your everyday life, as it will enable you to have much more control over negativity.

I have seen so many couples– including my own relationships– go through the initial euphoria of a new relationship, claiming, 'this is the one', 'this time it is different', 'we are so much in love'. Then normally three to six months later, it all begins to change, as low-vibrational energy finds its way into the relationship and starts to drag down the collective energy vibration of the two people. Then, before you know it, they have broken up or settled into a mid zone relationship with the magical sparkle becoming more of a dull shine. I am sure most of us have experienced or will experience this at some time in our lives. In fact, this is considered normal and generally accepted as what inevitably happens in relationships. The ones that stay together when they realise that they are in 'just another normal relationship' are usually tied in by responsibilities, children, financial constraints or are simply dependent on each other and feel it is better than being alone.

I'm not saying that when the relationship slips down to the mid zone that you should bale out, because you may have very important responsibilities, such as children to bring up, and many people are very happy in this type of relationship. What I am saying is that when the relationship drops down the vibrational scale, you are falling out of love, or moving away from the vibration of love.

Just because your relationship has dropped down the vibrational scale a little, away from the vibration of love, this does not mean that it has failed, because I believe that all relationships are teaching us about ourselves. Each relationship that you have is a valuable and important opportunity for personal growth.

What Causes Us to Fall Out of Love?

Low-vibrational energy causes us to fall out of love. It attacks us from the inside through our own personal insecurities, and can be triggered off by many different things, usually the behaviour of our partner or maybe through other external events and situations. Low-vibrational energy is energy of a slow vibration that causes our personal energy vibration to slow down and fall away from the vibration of the energy that we call love. It could be jealousy, envy, greed, selfishness, self-doubt, self-hate, anger or fear.

Personal insecurities

Every one of us carries our own low-vibrational thought patterns about ourselves and the world around us. These negative thoughts hold down the vibration of our personal energy frequency. As we looked at in the lives of Jeff and Dave (see page 30), these negative thoughts can be very damaging, to every area of our lives. If you can imagine a large metal bucket full of all the low-vibrational thoughts that you habitually carry about yourself and the world around you, then you can see how this acts as a dead weight holding you down and preventing your energy vibration from rising. This bucketful of negativity is extremely dangerous to your relationships and is always ready to surface and do untold damage. If you can imagine your inner child holding on to the bucket with a tight grip, then you can now see clearly that this bucket full of insecurities resides in the programme that your inner child runs your life by, the programme that was mainly put in place during the first five or six years of your life. When you were born you will have had few insecurities about yourself, but you gather these negative opinions through the ups and downs of life. Of course, these are unavoidable, but your upbringing determines just how severe your insecurities will be.

Let's say your parents never showed you any affection, never cuddled or kissed you. Then it would be no surprise if you grew up feeling unloved. This would become your programming and when later on in life you did receive love, you would find this very difficult to accept. Your inner child would try to pull you away from this source of love, to keep you down at the vibrational frequency at which it was programmed to believe you belong. Maybe your sister or brother received more attention than you did. This might result in your child becoming envious. This pattern can be carried throughout your life, ready to surface at any time, which can be very damaging to your relationships.

There are many scenarios that can occur and there are many other influential factors that have a bearing on determining your insecurities and the intensity of them. Your personality type, your genes and your temperament all affect how you will react to situations; we could all have exactly the same upbringing and yet come out with different amounts of insecurities.

Difficult relationships can make you insecure
You can also pick up many insecurities from your relationships. If you have a bad experience, such as a habitually unfaithful partner, then this would add to your

insecurities, as your trust has been shattered. The fact that your partner was unfaithful may well make you feel you are not deserving of love, as they were constantly saying to you by being unfaithful that they preferred somebody else to you. This can be very damaging to your self-esteem and result in you taking on board this negative programming. This makes your bucket of insecurities even heavier. Basically, insecurity is a negative way of viewing ourselves that affirms to us that we are not deserving of love.

The extent and intensity of our insecurities determines how far we will hold our personal energy vibration rate below the vibration of love. The heavier the bucket, the more it will pull you down. For example, if you have no insecurities you will love yourself 100 per cent. Now imagine that your bucket is 25 per cent full of insecurities about yourself; it's fair to assume that the bucket will pull you down to loving yourself 75 per cent. If your bucket was 50 per cent full, then you can see that you would be pulled down to 50 per cent loving yourself. This means the heavier your bucket, the more you will live your life through the insecurities contained within it.

In a worst case scenario you could end up living your entire life through the insecurities contained within your bucket, which would mean living full time with feelings such as worthlessness, fear, self-hate, jealousy, resentment and envy. These extremely negative and damaging thought patterns could become your everyday mantra. Some people spend their lives in this state and this is where drug addiction, alcoholism and even suicide are commonplace. This is a very low-vibrational zone.

Fortunately most of us don't have that heavy a bucket, which means that our insecurities will only occasionally be activated. Most of the time we can go through life without even knowing that they are there, then one day, often through a trivial action, they can be triggered. This is why the honeymoon period of a relationship doesn't last forever. The fact that we are in love and vibrating at the heights guarantees that any insecurities that we have will make an appearance sooner or later. The heavier the bucket, the faster this happens.

Negative energy pulls you down away from love, through your insecurities about yourself.

Insecurities take a while to surface

When you start a new relationship, your inner child is usually quiet for the first three months, as the excitement that this new person brings to your life is very entertaining for your inner child. In addition, your initial euphoria overrides your inner child for a while. Then, just like all children, eventually it grows bored and begins to be heard. This is when your troubles will begin. My experience has shown that this usually starts at around the three-month point and continues to rise in intensity over the following three months, so when your relationship reaches the six to nine-month stage negativity (your insecurities) can be taking a real hold (your inner child can be kicking and screaming). This is where you can find your energy vibration plummeting, as you find yourself falling out of love.

You often find that little things that your new partner tells you about themselves and their past may cause you a little niggle at first, but nothing more. Then as these little minor things build up over a period of time (three to six months), they appear more and more of a big deal. It could be something minor like how they behaved with a previous partner or maybe what they felt for them, or even telling a little white lie, that gives your bucket of insecurities a little shake. You see what appear to be minor insignificant irritations, that in themselves are hardly worth getting yourself worked up about collect in the recess of your subconscious mind.

Then suddenly one day it all comes out and you are engulfed with all the self-doubt that has built up inside of you and a small disagreement can erupt into a full-scale row. If you are not careful, this can be the beginning of the end and very difficult to climb back up from. This negative onslaught can eventually escalate until you actually find your relationship breaking apart. This can be particularly damaging if you are the rejected partner, as this can unearth even more of your deep-seated insecurities about yourself. To be rejected in a relationship affirms to your subconscious mind that you are not deserving of love, which compounds the situation even further making you feel even worse about yourself. This is why many break-ups are so difficult, and often depression can be part and parcel of the whole process. Of course, this three to nine-month timescale does not apply to everybody, but in my experience it has proved accurate on many occasions.

Back to the comfort zone

Your inner child is ingenious in finding ways to get what it wants and can be very persuasive when it wants to be. By falling in love you have in effect moved out of your comfort zone, and when this happens it's only a matter of time, before your inner child begins to attempt to pull you back in. You may be prone to jealousy, and if this is the case your inner child will use this potential weak link to try to drag you away from your partner and back into your comfort zone. A little voice within your mind will attempt to convince you that your partner maybe enjoying attention from elsewhere, when this may not be the case at all. Things can be blown out of all proportion and if you're not careful you can convince yourself of things that don't even exist. This is how manipulative your own subconscious mind can be. Be very careful when this happens, as you need to take a step back and reassess the situation.

A friend of mine was convinced that his wife was enjoying admiring glances from other men, which of course is not wrong. But what he felt was wrong was that she was reciprocating the looks back to the admirer. This made him feel very insecure and he truly believed that she was doing this, even though she denied that it was taking place. It came to a head one evening when I was actually present, and I was able to reassure my friend that he had seen something that hadn't actually happened. You see, his inner child (subconscious mind) felt threatened when his wife was around other men. This was due to past experiences and this fear had become logged into his subconscious programme. He actually feared it happening so much that he almost expected it to happen and even the slightest reason was enough for his inner child to start screaming, 'See, I told you so.' This fear, which he carried in his bucket of insecurities, was always ready to surface and would jump at any chance it could to validate itself. This is how our insecurities work.

You can guarantee that when you fall in love and your vibration rises, sooner or later your insecurities will come in to play and attempt to pull you back down. It's all about your programming. Your inner child will be quite content if it can successfully drag down your energy vibration and lead you into a mid zone, semi-dead relationship, as its only concern is to keep you in the frequency zone in which it believes you belong. Remember: your inner child cannot differentiate between what is good and bad for you. It just sticks to what it has been programmed to believe you deserve.

Selfish acts will take their toll

Selfishness is the most destructive component to your relationships, outside of yourself. How selfish your partner is will determine how fast this activates your bucket of insecurities. You may be a totally unselfish person who cares very deeply and is always thoughtful in respect of your partner, but this will be tested to the hilt if your partner is selfish. When your partner is selfish to you, this means they have put themselves before your feelings. Every act of selfishness towards you is a statement to your subconscious mind saying, 'I don't care about you.' If this negative affirmation is constantly replayed it will soon damage your relationship and drag down your vibration rate; it will eventually kill your love for your partner.

It could be something as simple as not returning a text message or making themselves a cup of coffee without bothering to ask if you want one that chips away at your love. Of course, even the most unselfish people will occasionally forget, but it's when this type of selfish behaviour becomes a habit that the real damage is being done. Being selfish to your partner is just constantly affirming to them that other things are more important than they are. A friend of mine is so unselfish she constantly puts other people before herself. I have seen her many times put herself out for other people, even though she hasn't wanted to do the things, or go to the places that they have pushed her into. If you have any insecurities about yourself– and that's 99 per cent of us– then selfishness will sooner or later bring them to the surface. This will drag down your relationship into the mid zone or even the low zone, losing that wonderful feeling of love that you could have enjoyed in the high zone.

What goes up always comes down

Falling in love guarantees one thing and that is, sooner or later, your insecurities will surface and attempt to sabotage your relationship. You see, if you have risen up the vibrational scale due to falling in love, then this is not a true high, as you are dependent on an external source, namely your partner, for this lift in vibration. To be truly in love you must rise up the vibrational scale without outside help, you must love yourself and you must carry no negative thoughts about yourself. Then and only then is it of a permanent nature.

How Do You Stay in Love?

The answer to this question is very simple: you must first learn to love yourself. Until you love yourself, accepting yourself totally for who you are and reaching the point where you have no insecurities about yourself whatsoever, you will always be carrying around with you your bucket of insecurities. This bucket is what does all the damage and as long as you carry it inside of you it will always be difficult for you to stay in the high zone. Your bucket will always pull down your energy vibration away from the frequency of love as long as you are holding on to it. This is why that wonderful feeling you have when you fall in love with somebody is, in 99 per cent of cases, only temporary. Don't despair, though, as through your relationship you can heal many of the insecurities that you are carrying. If you know what is taking place you can work at keeping your vibration rate at the higher levels.

A relationship is the best place to be to help you overcome your bucket of insecurities. If you enter a relationship and you are both only carrying a small number of insecurities, you have a very good chance of staying in love, if you understand what is taking place and learn how to deal with your insecurities when they arise. Every time an insecurity comes up, such as jealousy, you must deal with it, talk it through and don't let it take hold within your mind and fester, because if you let it take hold

To stay in love you must get rid of your insecurites about yourself so that you can rise back up the vibrational scale. You must love yourself more.

untold damage can be done. You must get things on the table immediately and clear the air. Take time to listen to your partner and remember that you can see things in a very biased way when your inner child is trying to manipulate your mind. Look at any problems that seem to be arising very carefully and remember your inner child can often convince you to see things that are not actually happening. You must have trust in each other and work this out together, as you are both facing the insecurities that you individually hold about yourselves. Helping each other work through your insecurities is a transformational experience that will have huge positive benefits for you both for the rest of your lives.

Love should come from within

To stay in love you have to attain the vibration of love, as an individual without any external help. Then and only then can you truly stay in love. Until you reach this point you will always have to rely on somebody else to boost your energy vibration rate. Relationships are not, as we often hope, the answer to all our problems as we feel at last we have found love and happiness; but they are a means to attaining that goal and offer us a wonderful opportunity for personal growth. In some cases, of course, the final stages of our journey are taken with another person in a relationship, and in these cases deep and true love can flourish.

Make sure you like yourself

If you have the following qualities, you are close to the vibration of love and blissful happiness is within your grasp. You have to be:

- totally unselfish, always putting other people before yourself;
- caring and considerate;
- loving and compassionate;
- trustworthy and honest;
- honourable and loyal;

‣ kind and thoughtful;
‣ sincere and genuine;
‣ strong and determined;
‣ forgiving and virtuous.

If you can attain all of these qualities then you will be very close to the vibration of love and your last remaining task is to let go of your bucket in order to enter into the blissful state that we call love. When you are at this stage, your final task is to let go of your bucket. This when a relationship can be just what you need to complete the task. This boost in love can give you the impetus to believe in yourself and let go of your remaining insecurities.

Be content
If you are feeling lonely and have a need to be with somebody then this is a sure sign that you are not yet ready for a relationship. You see, if you think you need somebody else to make you happy, then you are still carrying insecurities about yourself. It's when you feel totally comfortable being on your own and don't need somebody else to make you feel happy and content that you are truly ready. When you carry very few insecurities about yourself into a relationship, you will do little to damage it. When you least need it or even want it, is when you are ready. How ironic is that!

How Do You Get the Love Back into your Relationship?

If you have had the honeymoon period and feel that you have slid back down the vibrational scale, don't despair; there are things that you can do to raise your energy frequency back up. Remember that it is perfectly normal for this to happen, as without the knowledge of what takes place you have little chance of being able to stop this process. HVT can give you that knowledge and the tools to be able to take control, instead of events controlling you. You have to raise your energy field back up to the vibration of love and to do this you must relinquish the negative thought patterns that you have picked up about each other and yourself along the way.

A clean sheet
The first step in achieving this is to put the past behind you and give each other a clean sheet. Accept that from now on your relationship is going to be based on trust and total honesty. To hold on to any bad feelings from the past is just allowing low-vibrational thoughts to stay rooted within your mind, which will hold down your personal energy vibration, damaging nobody but yourself. You have to understand that anything that happened in the past was perpetrated by two people with little control over their own

thought processes and subject to the limitations that your own subconscious minds placed upon you. With a fresh start you can make a dedication to each other that confirms your commitment to the process of loving each other and improving your lives for the better.

Remember: if your energy vibration rate is held down at the lower levels, whatever you do in your life will be below your potential. This applies to every aspect of your life. If you can raise your energy vibration rate, your life will improve, so any work that you can do to improve your relationship will help every other area of your life. In effect, you are reprogramming yourself.

Support each other

You must help each other in your climb back up the mountain and offer support and love when needed. This will make the journey far more comfortable than attempting the climb alone. You have a unique opportunity to rise up together and this means you have more chance of achieving success with the constant support of each other. The prize that awaits you is far greater than you may realise, as this time when you attain the vibration of love it will be a much more lasting experience than the fleeting glimpse that you were given before. This is the only real and true path to love and to be able to share this journey with another is a wonderful opportunity.

Later in this book (see page 117), I will take you through a guided programme of exercises that will enable you individually and as a couple to rise back up the vibrational scale towards the energy that we call love.

How Do You Get Rid of your Bucket of Insecurities?

Your insecurities are the habitual negative thought patterns that you have about yourself that have the effect of permanently holding down the vibration of your personal energy field. To get rid of these very damaging thought patterns, you have to cleanse your subconscious mind and eradicate them from your thinking. You must reprogramme your subconscious mind with positive thoughts about yourself, which will help your personal energy vibration rise to the higher levels. It is your inner child (subconscious mind) that carries these thought patterns, so this is where your work must be focused. You have to teach your inner child to think differently and this will change your general perception of yourself and your personal expectations. Remember: whatever your inner child thinks you deserve in life is what you will get, keeping you within the confines of your comfort zone.

Insecurities can engulf you

Let's take a look at a real life example that I can give you of how your insecurities can surface with a vengeance.

Lucy was insecure and very sensitive, which meant she was prone to engaging negativity in respect of her relationships and this could be triggered off at anytime. She was open to the possibility of something going wrong, as her previous experiences had cast serious doubt as to whether she deserved love (high-vibrational energy) in her life. One particular incident happened when she telephoned her partner Mike (with whom she was very much in love) and he didn't answer his phone. It just went immediately on to answer phone. So she sent him a text message and he didn't reply. Starting to feel a little anxious, she sent him two further text messages, still to no avail. When 30 minutes had past and he still had not got back to her, she began to imagine all kinds of things. 'He must be with another woman,' she thought to herself. 'I mean, why else would he have his phone turned off? That's why he was behaving strangely today; he must be hiding something.' All this, even though he had reassured her earlier that he was just a bit tired because of a few drinks the night before. A few more minutes passed and she was fully engaging this negative frenzy within her mind, which was of course dragging down the vibration of her energy field. She was becoming angry and hurt. How could he do this to her, when she loved him so much? She could never trust another man again.

Unnecessary damage can be done

Meanwhile Mike was snuggled up in bed, drinking his hot chocolate, enjoying the television, oblivious to her dilemma. 'Ah,' he thought to himself. 'I'm feeling tired now. I'll send my lovely Lucy a goodnight text then settle down for a good night's sleep.' As he was sending the text message he heard his phone bleep. 'Oh, Lucy must be texting me goodnight at the same time. That's nice,' he thought.

When he had finished, he opened her message and read, 'WHY HAVEN'T YOU REPLIED TO ME?' 'That's odd', he thought. 'I haven't received a message. I'd better phone her to see what's up.'

Well, he never expected what came next. A tirade of anger and accusations poured down the phone and no matter how hard he tried to reassure her, she was having none of it. She was adamant. There were no possible excuses; he had his phone turned off because he was up to something? Why else would he do that? He tried to explain that it must have been the phone signal that was down and maybe that's why she couldn't get through, but she wouldn't listen and slammed the phone down.

This continued throughout the next day and their relationship was suffering, as the mass of negative feelings and emotions took their toll. Both of their energy fields were dragged down the vibrational scale and suddenly they were looking at each other in a different way. What was once a beautiful high zone relationship was now way down at the bottom of the mid zone or even entering the low zone.

Doubt can fester in your mind

They eventually made up and she accepted that she may have got things a little wrong and hopefully no long-term damage had been done. The danger here is that the incident may have created doubt in her mind that she might never fully recover from, which would result in their relationship to some degree slipping down the vibrational scale on a permanent basis. This is how it works and all of the little negative incidents add up, eventually dragging down the relationship away from love. This is how you fill up your bucket of insecurities.

If Lucy had no insecurities she would have handled the situation totally differently. When Mike phoned her, she would probably have said, 'Oh hello, darling. I have been trying to get in touch with you, but your phone was off. I hope everything is OK.' All of the pain came from inside her, creating a totally unnecessary situation that was stressful and damaging to both of them.

This is how we usually tear our relationships apart and it's all due to our bucket of insecurities. That little voice in your head can convince you of things that aren't even there. You can imagine all kinds of scenarios, which can be very damaging to your personal energy frequency and your relationship. Just imagine a five-year-old child whinging on upset, trying to convince you that something must be wrong. This is exactly what is happening, only it's your inner child that is doing the complaining. When you don't know how it works, it's very easy to take those thoughts as your own and you can soon be completely sure that what you're imagining is the absolute truth.

We are all subject to this manipulation by our subconscious mind and it is simply our inner child's way of keeping us within our comfort zone. It doesn't want us to get too happy, because this would raise our personal energy vibration to a level higher than it is programmed to believe we deserve to be. When we fall in love we rise in vibration, which moves us out of our comfort zone, so it is only a matter of time before our subconscious mind begins the process to pull us back down.

Reprogramming is the answer

To change your programming and get rid of your personal insecurities you have to learn how to handle your inner child when it starts to moan. You need to use proven methods of child handling, to educate and reassure your inner child, in order to transmute the negativity present. This negativity is the sum total of all the hurt and pain that you have suffered in your life, which states you are not deserving of love. This can include:

▶ being neglected as a child;
▶ being told your are stupid, ugly, worthless, silly or daft;
▶ not being shown much affection;

▶ not being given any responsibility;
▶ not being praised or acknowledged for your
  achievements.

In fact anything negative that you encounter in your life,
especially in your early years, contributes to this belief that
you are not deserving of love. This is a belief that we all
carry to some degree, and these negative affirmations
damage us and can accumulate, making our bucket heavier
and heavier.

Step aside from negativity

Next time you feel your insecurities begin to surface, you
must understand that it is your inner child starting to
complain in order to drag you back into your comfort

*Learning how to handle your inner child when it starts trying
to drag you down is a very effective way of eradicating your
insecurities, but you can also work on this when you are in a
normal state of mind. You do this through visualisation.*

zone. You must not engage the negativity that your inner child is trying to ensnare you with. Do not allow yourself to be taken over by anger, jealousy, hate or resentment. Just as you would with a real child, allow your inner child to have its tantrum, but remain unaffected by the drama. Let the negative feelings take their course, observe them but remain detached from them. When you engage the negativity you validate the energy and add to the bucket, rather than detract from it. When your inner child has vented its fury and settled down, then through visualisation (see page 105) you can carry out a comforting exercise, reassuring your inner child that you love and cherish it. Again, as with a real child, when your inner child realises that its tantrums have no effect, it will stop having them; but when you react to them the child continues to use this method to get what it wants.

If you engage the negativity that your inner child is using to try to drag you back down, you will find that you attract events and situations that resonate at the same frequency. In other words, if you become angry you will find yourself attracting angry situations to yourself. In Lucy's case, she became angry with Mike so he became angry back with her, which resulted in them arguing and becoming fully immersed in the negativity present. This strengthens the anger within them both, adding to their buckets of insecurities. Engaging any form of negativity simply affirms to us that we are, in terms of our energy vibration, at the level that we believe we deserve. Those who are enlightened never engage negativity and are therefore never dragged down from the vibration of love, because truly enlightened people have no insecurities. If anger is not in your bucket of insecurities, then you won't get angry; if jealousy is not in your bucket of insecurities then you won't get jealous; and so on.

Practical Steps to Help You Fall Back in Love

Falling out of love is something that most of us will experience at sometime in our lives and probably more than once. It is perfectly natural for this to happen and virtually impossible to avoid, such is the nature of our world. Up until now we have had little control over this and were simply subject to this inevitable process running its course. An understanding of HVT gives you the tools to help you negotiate your way through the incredibly complex emotional experience that we call a relationship. Without such tools, your chances of success are slim. You would probably go through one relationship after another repeating the same mistakes and failing to learn the valuable lessons that they afford us. Without being able to learn and improve as we go along, we are going to make very limited progress towards keeping our relationships in the high zone.

Work together

Using HVT and working with your partner is the best way to get the most from your relationship and ensure that you give it the best chance of survival. Survival in this case means keeping the vibration of your relationship at the highest possible level. HVT can give you the tools to climb back up the vibrational scale and move back into the high zone: in other words, to fall back in love. This is because HVT empowers you to be in control of the low-vibrational events and situations that normally control you. This means you will sustain less damage when confronted by the negativity. You will understand why and how you manage to fall out of love, empowering you with the ability to handle your insecurities in a much more beneficial way.

Working with your partner is vitally important if you are to make real progress, and an agreement between you is essential as the basis for making real headway within your relationship. If you both read this book and come to an understanding of HVT, you will be able to work together and help each other along the way. All past negativity needs to be released, so that you can both make a fresh start with a clean sheet. You both need to agree that what is past is past and you are prepared to start again from scratch. This clearing of the past is an act of forgiveness of each other and mentally prepares you for your climb back to love.

You must understand that you both will have been subject to your insecurities and without the knowledge of HVT you will have had little control over the negativity generated. This will have caused many of the niggles and problems that you will both have had. It's a bit like sailing along in a boat without a rudder and being subject to the flow of the river and currents. Sometimes it may be calm and peaceful and other times you could be tossed around by the rapids with no sense of control whatsoever. I believe HVT provides you with a rudder and enables you to negotiate your way through your relationship.

Commitment

You must both make a commitment to be totally honest
with each other and not to allow any form of mistrust to
creep in and weaken the fabric of your relationship. You
must be very open and have a no secrets policy in order for
this to work, otherwise low-vibrational energy will find a
way in. I would suggest that initially you take it one day
at a time, setting aside an assessment period of, say, 20
minutes each evening to reflect on how your day has gone.
This provides an opportunity for you both to clear the air if
anything has bothered you. This is very therapeutic and
essential if your are to disperse any low-vibrational energy
that may be lurking with your minds. To leave this
unattended would allow the negativity to take a stronger
hold and at worst become permanently rooted within your
mind, adding more weight to your bucket of insecurities,
dragging down your relationship in the process.

**Now let's take a hypothetical look at how a couple
might find their relationship is affected, when they
understand how HVT works.**

Anne and Ian were a couple that decided to use HVT to
help put the love back into their relationship. They felt that
they could work together and saw the potential for
personal growth in this joint commitment. Their
relationship up to that point had been fairly typical. They
had been together for one year and both agreed that the
sparkle had diminished somewhat. Ian worked as the
assistant manager for an electrical goods shop and Anne
worked as a clerical assistant for the council.

When they first met, they had hit it off immediately
and seemed meant for each other. The first three months
were hectic as they saw more and more of each other,
enjoying meals out and fun nights in. It was a very happy
period for both of them. They enjoyed each other's
company so much that they hardly ever went out without

each other. Their old friends hardly ever saw them, as they spent all of their time together. They talked openly about their previous relationships and both appeared to be comfortable with each other's past.

The first signs of insecurities surfacing

Then one day after they had been together approximately three months they had their first disagreement. Anne had always had some problems in her family, as her brother sometimes got himself in trouble with the police. It was nothing too serious: just minor traffic offences, although once he had been prosecuted for stealing a car. However, he was always short of money and more often than not Anne would be handing him cash. She went on to Ian over and over about her brother and how she wished he could just get a job and stop being such a burden. Now, Ian had heard all this before but this time he had just had enough, he snapped back at Anne, telling her it was her own fault for been so soft with him. She didn't take this criticism too well, and a row erupted that resulted in them not speaking to each other for several days.

Eventually they made up, but things were slowly taking a turn for the worse; he blamed her and she blamed him. Negativity had slowly but surely found its way in and because neither would accept any fault, they both held on to some low-vibrational thoughts and feelings. Ian resented the way that Anne had treated him over the incident and this negative feeling had triggered off his insecurities, which simply confirmed to him that obviously she can't love him that much. This dragged down the vibration of his energy field and pulled him into a lower vibrational zone. Anne felt the same she was upset at the way Ian had spoken to her and this had triggered off her insecurities, dragging down her vibrational frequency in the process.

Things can appear different

This meant that now their relationship had slipped down slightly and they began to see each other in a totally different way. Both of their subconscious minds were having a field day, seizing every opportunity to reaffirm their insecurities. Of course, there were many other minor incidents that had chipped away at their vibration level, but this was the straw that broke the camel's back. Relatively minor incidents that to this point had been overlooked, such as been late, forgetting to telephone, listening to their personal problems over and over or being taken for granted, came rushing to the fore. All the little things that had mounted up exploded out and the disagreement had acted as the trigger.

Falling out of love

All of a sudden the desire to be together all the time didn't seem to be so attractive. They started to spend more time apart and soon fell back into their old routines with their pals. When you are in a lower vibrational zone you don't even look the same to each other. The magic sparkle has gone and you start to see faults. The next thing they knew, they had been together for seven months and they had woken up in just another normal relationship. Without the knowledge of HVT they had no idea what had caused them to fall out of love. They just knew that the magic had gone and that what they'd had had somehow disappeared.

Using HVT to rise back to the vibration of love

Learning the principals of HVT put everything into perspective, they now understood what had happened to them and they could see things much more clearly. They were amazed at how little control they had previously had within their relationship and realised without that control the relationship was doomed from the start. It really was like been adrift without a rudder– and what chance do any of us have in that position? They felt empowered by HVT and decided to work together to put things right. They made a commitment to each other and forgave each other for previous selfish acts, which gave them a clean sheet and a fresh start.

Every evening they would discuss their day and talk through any niggles or problems that they felt were arising. For example, Anne was slightly upset that Ian hadn't sent her a text message one lunchtime as he usually did. She thought at first he must be busy, and then her thoughts changed to, 'Maybe he isn't so bothered about me now' and 'He has forgotten because I am not that important to him.' These thought patterns opened up her insecurities and before long she became agitated and distraught at his apparent lack of concern for her. Her energy vibration plummeted and she felt bad about herself and their relationship. Eventually she decided to ring him and voice her concerns. She wasn't happy and told him so. 'I don't think you feel the same way about me,' she said. 'I just want honesty like we agreed and to be told if you are tired of our relationship.' He tried to explain: 'But I was in an important meeting and I am sorry,' but Anne was having none of it and repeated her concerns. When the phone went down Ian felt dejected and unhappy: 'I don't need this in my life, he thought to himself, and his energy field dropped down in vibration.

Discussion works

Later that evening when they had their discussion time Anne realised that in fact Ian had done nothing wrong and had simply been busy at work. This should have been perfectly understandable, as his job can be very demanding. She also understood that the real problem was her insecurities, which had blown everything out of proportion. Her subconscious mind had seized the opportunity to flood her mind with doubt and she had without realising fully engaged it. This brought all of her fears to the surface, and just because a simple text message had not arrived, in no time at all she had convinced herself that he didn't care about her any more. Fortunately they now had a good understanding of how it all works and were able to face up to their responsibility in the incident and release the negativity that had taken hold. Ian apologised for not being able to text her and said he should have foreseen the possibility of the meeting going on longer than expected. Next time he would always let her know when he was going into a meeting, so she could understand if it happened again. She apologised for her reaction and accepted that the pain she had felt came from inside of her. He had not hurt her, but simply provided the trigger to set it all off.

Using HVT is empowering

Their ability to understand what was happening had allowed them both to let go of the bad feelings generated and prevent this negative situation from taking a permanent hold within their minds. It's small, seemingly insignificant incidents like this that occur most days of our lives and given time are so damaging to the vibration of our relationships. All the little things add up and slowly pull us down from the vibration of love. HVT puts you in control, and as long as you deal with each little negative incident as they arise, you can prevent them adding up and destroying your love for each other. Handling the negatives in your life keeps you vibrating at the higher levels.

You can use HVT yourself

Even if your partner shows no interest in HVT and refuses to work with you on your relationship, you can still make huge strides on your own. Your understanding of what is taking place in your relationship will grow, as you see things in a new and very empowering way. You will have more control over the inevitable negative events and situations that will arise, allowing you the opportunity for personal growth.

It is inevitable that our insecurities will surface at some point in our relationships and it is something that most of us will have to face. Even in the best high zone relationships, your insecurities will make themselves heard sooner or later. When this happens you must ride them out, and then accept your part in the situation and in the process be totally honest about your role. Handling this in the correct way is essential if you are to clear away any negativity and not allow it a foothold in your relationship.

I see it as a three-step process:

Step one: Ride the rapids
You are taken over by your insecurities and dragged into a vortex of negativity. You may become upset and angry, jealous and insecure or feel hurt and let down. Whatever the pain that you feel, you have an opportunity to disengage from the attempts of your inner child to draw you in, and allow it to blow itself out.

As discussed earlier (see page 83), you must handle your inner child in the right way.

Next time you feel your insecurities begin to surface you must understand that it is your inner child complaining in order to drag you back into your comfort zone. You must not engage with this negativity. You must allow your inner child to have its tantrum but remain unaffected by the drama, just as you would with a real child. You must allow the negative feelings to take their course whilst not allowing them to engage you; observe them but remain detached. When your inner child has vented its fury and settled down, carry out a comforting visualisation exercise (see page 105) to reassure your inner child that you love and cherish it. When your inner child realises that its tantrums have no effect on you, it will stop having them.

Step two: Learn to say sorry
Allow things to settle down by allowing your vibration rate to rise gently back to close to its normal level, letting go of the negative thoughts and feelings that have dragged you down. Then make your apologies to each other, which will encourage a further letting go of negativity. You must be genuine in your apology, because holding on to any bad feeling is simply going to ensure that your relationship sustains long-term, and possibly permanent, damage. It is vital at this stage that you work together to clear the air as much as possible.

Step three: Be honest
This is often the most difficult stage, but it is also the most powerful in terms of clearing away some of those insecurities for good. You must be totally honest with yourself and accept your part in the whole episode. You must be able to look yourself in the mirror and admit when you are wrong. Accepting responsibility is an immensely powerful transformational tool. It stops the low-vibrational energy from taking permanent hold and adding to your bucket of insecurities. You need to talk about the situation and be brutal in your assessment of your part in it. It is likely that you will find that you both played a role in allowing negativity to take hold and pull down your energy vibration. It's very difficult to resist the low-vibrational energy when your insecurities surface, so don't be too disappointed when this happens. What is important is that you understand what is happening when

it takes place, and this observation is in itself is a big step towards gaining an element of control and moving up the vibrational scale.

Teamwork

I believe working with your partner as a team and talking things through gives you a much deeper understanding of what is taking place, than if you attempt this analysis alone. This presents a wonderful opportunity for you both and you can individually take huge strides forward in your personal development. If your relationship it isn't working very well, you don't realise what a treasure-chest of fine jewels and riches it could be; and even if you do realise it, you don't have a key to open it. HVT is that key and gives you access to more riches than you ever dreamed, far more valuable than diamonds, gold and jewels. Everything that you ever dreamed of is available to you, if you can rid yourself of your insecurities and allow your energy vibration to align itself with the vibration of love.

Tips to Help Lift the Vibration of your Relationship

In this section, I am going to look at a number of easy, practical ideas you can incorporate into your daily life to help you keep your relationship at a high-energy level.

Keep a happy box

Remembering the good times that you have had together is a good way of instantly changing your thoughts, from low-vibrational to high-vibrational. When you hit the low times and low-vibrational energy is clawing away at you, you may find it helpful if you can develop methods to take your mind off the negativity.

Keep a happy box, maybe an old shoe box, and keep all your positive memorabilia in there. Save birthday cards, Christmas cards, gift tags from presents, theatre tickets, cinema tickets, everything that you can that made you feel good about your relationship.

Look through your collection of photographs and pick out the happy ones where you were both enjoying yourselves and place them around your home, car, and if possible place of work.

Keep a positive diary and record in it all the good times that you have. Write down the fine details: how you felt, if you were happy, the emotions present, any compliments that your partner gave you. Put down everything: if you went for a romantic meal write down what you ate, what your partner ate, how you enjoyed the evening. If your partner sends you flowers keep the card and record your feelings describing how you felt when you received them.

Whenever you feel down go, through your happy things and picture how you felt then, and allow the positive, contented feelings come back to you as the negativity slips away. Sometimes you can forget how wonderful and lovely your partner really is and it helps to be able to remind yourself of that occasionally.

Be impulsive

Be spontaneous. Things that haven't been planned in advance often turn out to be the most enjoyable. Make it a habit to surprise your partner with new ideas and make your lives exciting in the process. Maybe jump on a train and go out for the day; don't plan where, just see where it takes you. Have a night away without planning it; just get in the car and off you go. Take a bus into town and have a nice lunch, followed by a few drinks. Break your routine and you will be surprised how alive it makes you feel. Try lots of new things: ice-skating, swimming, bowling, cycling, walking, painting, tennis, golf. Sleep under the stars. Paddle in the sea. All this will all encourage excitement and boost the vibration of your relationship.

You are in effect entertaining your inner child and if you can do this your energy vibration will rise. You know what children are like when they get bored; they become lethargic, whingy and tiresome. So when your life is a monotonous routine, you are just dragging a bored inner child around with you. You are carrying a bundle of negativity that pulls you down into a lower vibrational zone. If you can get your inner child excited, you will release all of that negativity and your vibration will rise.

Compliment each other

Make a point of complimenting each other as often as possible and make a pact not to make negative comments about each other. This may take a little practice, but stay with it and as you reprogramme your subconscious mind and change your thinking process, you will boost your partner's confidence and increase your energy vibration. In your daily assessment session, point out any negative comments so that you can both be aware of how you are thinking and this will help you to change your ways. Often things can be said without you realising and unless they are pointed out you would never be aware of them. This monitoring of each other will be a very positive step forward and extremely beneficial to your relationship.

Send a love letter

The old-fashioned art of letter writing seems to have almost been forgotten in these days of e-mails and text messaging, but it is a wonderfully romantic way of telling your partner how much you love them. There is something quite magical about receiving a love letter from your partner and it is something that can be added to your happy box. It can give you many moments of pleasure reading it over and over again and it will constantly affirm to you that you deserve love. Find some nice writing paper and envelopes and put your feelings down on paper. You will be amazed what a positive exercise it is for you both. When something is written from the heart you can feel the love behind the words, and it becomes a high-vibrational package that you can access at any time.

Buy a present

Choose a little gift for your partner. It doesn't have to be expensive; it really is the thought that counts. Maybe a cuddly toy or an item of clothing and wrap it up for them to open. The fact that you have bothered to wrap the gift shows that they are worth the effort and is a confirmation that they deserve your love. Attach a card to it and write a nice message, a further affirmation that they deserve love in their life. This small, kind gesture will boost your partner's vibration and make you feel better about yourself into the bargain.

Be affectionate

Show your partner that you love them by holding their hand, kissing them, stroking their hair, hugging them, telling them how much you love them. Don't worry what other people think; just enjoy your love together and never be afraid to show it. Demonstrating your love to your partner, especially in public, is a very positive affirmation to them that you truly love them. This is a big confidence boost and has very good implications for your energy vibration rate.

Pamper night

Treat your partner to a pamper night. Prepare a nice, hot, bubble bath, complete with candles, and bring them a chilled glass of wine while they are soaking in the tub. Buy some nice bath foam and some quality moisturising creams and even a nice new set of nightwear. This could be followed with a romantic candlelit meal that you have prepared. All of this says that you love and care about your partner and promotes a feeling of togetherness, which melts away any negative energy that may be present.

Play your music

Music is a wonderful way of remembering the high-vibrational times and raising your energy vibration. You will have your favourite songs that mean something to your relationship, so play them when you feel negativity taking hold to help you to rise back up. Making your partner a tape or CD with all of your favourite songs on shows that you care and confirms your love for them. A thoughtful gift like this can be much more beneficial for your relationship than many expensive presents.

You must work at it

Keeping your relationship alive and exciting is very important in respect of staying in the high zone, in love, as this keeps your inner child entertained and happy. The more that you work at promoting positive things within your relationship, the more your insecurities will slowly disappear. You will be reprogramming your subconscious mind and you will be helping each other along the way. Your old negative habits and thought patterns will be replaced by new, positive thought patterns, and the effects will be felt throughout your life. Everything will work out better for you, be it relationships, work or leisure. You will feel the benefits of raising your energy vibration.

We live in an amazing world full of adventure and beauty, but if we are not careful we are so busy floundering around in the lower vibrational zones that we will miss out. Take one day at a time and enjoy this wonderful world of ours, because it will be over before you know it.

Affirmations

Affirmations are powerful statements that you repeat to yourself over and over, until eventually your subconscious mind (inner child) accepts them as being true. In effect, you are reprogramming your subconscious mind thus redefining the boundaries of your comfort zone. Use powerful, high-vibrational statements tailored to your own particular needs to replace low-vibrational thought patterns, raising the frequency of your personal energy field. The longer you keep this up, the more permanent the rise in frequency will be. Remember: the higher the vibration of your personal energy field, the better your relationship will be.

Affirmations should be written in the present tense as if you have already attained them and I would recommend that you read them to yourself, preferably out loud, every morning and every night just before you go to sleep. Each statement should be read 10 times, and you can keep repeating your favourite ones to yourself all day long, whenever you can find the time.

You will be amazed at how different you feel, after just a couple of weeks. The high-vibrational statements will be raising the frequency of your personal energy field. However, if after three to four weeks you feel that it's not really working anymore, don't be discouraged, because this is a crucial point at which you must keep up the bombardment. Your subconscious mind can be very clever and will use all its cunning persuasive powers to resist change, so it is important that you keep going. After six weeks, you will be making progress and the boundaries of your comfort zone will be changing without you realising it. At this point you may want to change some of your statements or even take some time out before you begin your next six-week course of affirmations. Here are some examples that you might use:

▶ I love and approve of myself.
▶ My relationship is healthy and high-vibrational.
▶ My partner and I are very positive to each other.

You could write them on flash cards and keep them in your purse or wallet or stick them on your fridge; in fact, place them anywhere that you will see them as you go about your daily business.

Believe me, you can't bombard your subconscious mind (inner child) enough. You should live and breathe high-vibrational thoughts and they will push up the frequency of your personal energy field, changing your life for the better in the process. It's very simple: the more high-vibrational thoughts that you think, the more used to it your mind will become. In effect, you are drowning out the low-vibrational thoughts and not allowing them to take hold and drag down your personal energy frequency. If you do this enough your subconscious mind will accept that this is the norm for you and then this will become your natural state of being.

High-vibrational statements raise your energy vibration rate, moving you closer to the frequency of love, making you feel better and making life much easier in the process. This will help keep your relationship in the high zone and closer to the energy of love.

Visualisation

Walt Disney said, 'If you can dream it, you can do it.' That is what visualisation is all about. Visualisation is a powerful tool that you can use to help reprogramme your subconscious mind. What you are doing is convincing your subconscious that you are capable of achieving the subject of your visualisation. The secret to success in any area of life is to believe that you can do it, or, to be more precise, to make your subconscious mind believe that you can do it. As the real source of your unlimited potential lies within your subconscious mind this is where your true capabilities lie.

Belief is the key to success, as truly to believe eliminates any doubts from your mind and moves you into a frequency zone where anything is possible. This is the zone where you are calm, happy and detached from the outcome of your objective. Becoming over-involved could open the door to doubt and pull your frequency level down into a less productive zone. The secret is to relax, know that you will succeed and trust in your ability. Just enjoy the moment and bask in the high vibrations. Then, almost without thinking about your objective, allow everything to flow naturally. success will be almost guaranteed.

These visualisation exercises will help you to eliminate any negative energy you may be holding on to and protect you from any new negative energy you may come across, enabling you to relax into the feeling of serenity and

Visualisation can help you to mould your expectations to your advantage.

happiness that the high-frequency zone brings with it and trust that everything will work out well for you.

How to visualise

A visualisation is nothing more complicated than a high-powered daydream! You simply need to get comfortable relax and give yourself completely to your imagination. Learn to see yourself as a person in a happy and fulfilling relationship, and this will become your comfort zone. The more you use visualisation, the better you will become at it and the easier it will be for your subconscious to accept the visualisation as real.

Comfort your inner child visualisation

Before I start I would like to point out that this exercise can sometimes unearth some very emotional issues from the past and of course that is what we are trying to achieve, but if you feel in any way apprehensive then it may be best to have somebody sit with you for the first few times that you engage in this visualisation. As they can be on hand to offer support and reassurance, if you feel this may be necessary.

Read through the exercise first, then get yourself comfortable and close your eyes, slowly running through it again in your mind. Alternatively, you and your partner can take turns reading it to each other.

The visualisation

Close your eyes and relax. Now imagine you are at the top of a lighthouse looking out of the windows across the calm sea. You can see boats and ships in the distance dancing, gently on the calm waves. It's a beautiful day, the sun is bright and there is a very gentle breeze. Now turn around and look behind you. There is an old wooden door leading to a stone spiral staircase. Open the door and listen to it creak as you pull it open. Step forward and begin to make your way down the stairs. One step at a time– you have to be careful because the stairs are old and worn– you slowly work your way down, round and round, and at last you reach the bottom.

There at the bottom is a child of about five years old, sitting on a huge, old rocking chair. The child looks up at you. Its face lights up as it sees who you are. Yes, it's you, your inner child, you at five years old. You reach down and pick up the child in your arms, giving it a big cuddle, and you see the look of joy spread across its face.

You whisper to the child, 'I'm sorry. I didn't even know you were here. But don't worry, I will never neglect you again. I will always be with you every day. I will look after you and take care of you. I love you very much.'

You open the huge door of the lighthouse and walk out into the beautiful sunshine. Your inner child wants to play and is eager to run on the beach. You put your inner child on to the sand and it runs off, kicking sand into the air. You run after it, also kicking sand into the air. You both run through the shallow water, splashing each other and giggling as you run. You see a nice rock to sit on where you can watch your inner child play. Your child is so happy running through the water and full of the joys of spring. Now your child comes over to you and you pick it up and cuddle it again. Tell your child that everything is going to be great from now on. Tell it you will always be there for it and you can visit the beach anytime it wants. Tell the child that you love it very much.

Remember: the point of this exercise is to see your inner child happy and having fun, and most of all to reassure it that you love it. Loving your inner child will help you release any deep-seated low-vibrational thought patterns that may be embedded within your mind.

Continue that type of visualisation whenever you feel the need. You can, of course, use your imagination to think of many different places you can visit with your inner child.

Building a relationship with your inner child

Comforting your inner child is an important exercise and very beneficial in many areas of your life. Firstly, it will have the effect of letting your inner child know that you are acknowledging its presence, and secondly it will help to release any low-vibrational thought patterns that may be rooted deep within your subconscious mind. They may have been there for many years, causing your personal energy frequency to be held down unnecessarily low. It is very important when trying to move your life forward that you clear out these low-frequency feelings and emotions. Otherwise, it's like carrying a dead weight and severely hampers your progress.

Now that you have made contact with your inner child, you may find it beneficial to keep up the relationship, and

Comforting your inner child shows it that you love it; when your inner child feels loved, it will be much more helpful to you as you negotiate life's hurdles.

visualisation is a wonderful way of doing this. As you start to use HVT in your life, you will become more aware of the constant tussle between your conscious and subconscious mind. When you feel this, it might help to take a little time to explain to your subconscious mind what it is that you are trying to achieve. Make your inner child part of your life; your life will be a lot easier if you can enlist its support in your endeavours. Explain to it the potential benefits to both of you and don't forget it is a child, so make it an attractive proposition. For example, you might be going through a difficult patch in your relationship and feeling a little insecure. Take time to explain to your inner child that you need to let go of your doubts and that this will help to lift your relationship back up the vibrational scale. Tell your child that you will treat it if it helps you to let go of the negative thoughts. Maybe you will get a new DVD or a box of chocolates. Remember that you are trying to motivate a five-year-old child.

Learning to communicate with your inner child is important if you are to move forward and fully realise your amazing potential. After all, it is the thought patterns that are programmed into the mind of your inner child that control and dominate your life, and the best way to make changes in this area is first of all to open the channels of communication.

Visualisation for entering the high-vibrational zone

The high-vibrational zone is that state of mind where low-vibrational energy is virtually non-existent. This is when you are capable of amazing achievements and can fulfil your true potential. You have taken control of your subconscious mind and instead of it placing its programmed limitations on your life, you have harnessed its incredible power and are using it for your benefit. To do this you must override your programming and convince your subconscious mind to let go of that damaging bucket of insecurities, so that you can achieve amazing things.

When you are in this state of mind, life begins to look totally different and a beautiful feeling of serenity and happiness engulfs you. You are floating in the moment and aware of how blissfully calm and peaceful life is. Whatever you are doing seems to take place effortlessly and you feel at one with your surroundings. You don't have to think too much, as your main focus is the overwhelming feeling of peace and tranquillity that pervades the very essence of your entire being. This is the feeling that you must hold on to, this is when you have no insecurities about yourself and are vibrating very close to the frequency of love.

You allow your self to function whilst almost being the observer, slightly to one side from the events taking place. You are not operating through your conscious mind; it is not making the decisions and it feels as if you are on autopilot as your subconscious takes over. The trick is to learn to float in this state without your conscious mind clicking back in and taking over. This enables your subconscious mind to stay in control and keep you in the high-frequency zone. To initiate this state, you must make your subconscious mind believe that it has no insecurities and this will eradicate negative thoughts from your mind. Belief is the inherent key, as this will eliminate any doubts from your mind, closing the door on low-vibrational energy. Your energy field will rise accordingly, moving you into the blissful all-empowering high-frequency zone. If you can believe it, you can achieve it, or, to be exact, if you can make your subconscious mind believe it, you can achieve it.

The following short visualisation exercise can be used to put yourself in the high-frequency zone. This can be used to prepare for your day or for a specific situation that you might have in mind, or to let go of any negativity that may be attempting to engage you.

The visualisation

Get yourself comfortable and relax. Take a couple of minutes to drift into a calm and serene state. For the moment, take out of your mind any problems that you've been pondering over and focus on your objective. I want you to make contact with your inner child again and explain to your inner child that you are going to let it be in control today and you will be on hand for support if it's needed. Reassure your inner child that you love it and explain that you will have only positive thoughts today and everything will work out perfectly. See your inner child's face as it takes in what you say. Remember that your objective is to make your inner child believe in what you are saying. There must be no doubts whatsoever; your inner child must totally believe in your words. Now I want you to repeat the following statement to your inner child 10 times, focus on the words and feel the meaning behind them as you absorb them into your being.

'I am having a totally positive day. My energy field is in the high-frequency zone and I feel calm, relaxed, peaceful, stress-free and in total control. I love this serene feeling of happiness that I have and I am going to stay in this beautiful state for the entire day. I can do anything; I just have to believe it.'

Still in your relaxed state, close your eyes and imagine that you are standing on a thick glass disc approximately one metre (three feet) across. This disc is the floor of a glass cylinder and the ceiling of this cylinder is also a thick glass disc. This cylinder protects you, as any low-vibrational energy that is directed at you simply bounces off this fully enclosed protective shield.

Now I want you to picture a brilliant beam of white light shining through the cylinder right down to the centre of the earth and up above you into the sky. The beam shines right through your body, lighting you up as if you are luminous, and dislodges any dark patches of negativity that you may be carrying. See the patches of dark, sludgy, negative energy collect in your stomach and when all the negative sludge is here, see your stomach open and let the sludge pour out into your bucket. This is all of your insecurities that you have been carrying about yourself that have accumulated throughout your life.

In front of you there is a handle on the window of the glass cylinder. Reach out, take the handle and slide open the window. Now throw out your bucket of insecurities and watch as it floats off into space. Close your window and relax, feeling secure as you bask in the powerful rays of the beam of white light as it penetrates and refreshes your entire being.

Now imagine yourself travelling down this beam of light to the centre of the earth and see that the beam comes to a stop in a deep granite cave. See that there are large bolts securing this beam of brilliant light to the floor of the cave. Now tighten these bolts as tight as you can with a giant socket set. Then you travel up the beam of light far into the sky, where you see that the beam stops in a white crystal cave. Again the beam is fastened into the roof of the crystal cave with large bolts. Take out your giant socket set and tighten up the bolts as tight as you can. Float back down to your cylinder and see yourself fully protected by this impregnable shield and firmly rooted to the earth and the sky. This shield protects you from any low-vibrational energy and keeps you safe and firmly secure in the high-frequency zone.

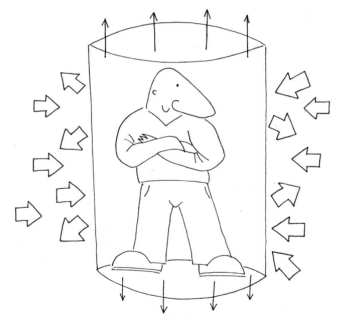

Your protective cylinder will help you repel low-vibrational energy.

This visualisation exercise will clear you of any insecurities and negative energy that you may be holding on to and protect you from any new negative energy that you may come across. You need to relax into the feeling of serenity and happiness that the high-frequency zone brings with it and trust that everything will work out well for you. Keep a careful eye on how you react throughout the day. Be aware that if any negative thoughts try to take hold, you can use your protective shield to repel them. Just go with the flow, as this will ensure that your subconscious mind remains in control and free from doubts (which are, of course, insecurities). If you can maintain this practice you will find that you remain in the high-vibrational zone, and this will ensure that whatever you do will be at the peak of your ability.

Face Your Fears

'You can gain strength, experience and confidence by every experience where you really stop to look fear in the face...You must do the thing you cannot do.' Eleanor Roosevelt

Your fears are like fences, you have to jump over them to find new territory. Facing your fears is a very powerful way of reprogramming your subconscious mind. The very reason that you perceive something as fearful or daunting is quite simply that you are feeling the apprehension of your subconscious mind, as you threaten to push out of the boundaries of your comfort zone. You might feel this fear as a welling up in your stomach as your mind fills with doubts at the thought of your up and coming challenge. It could literally be anything that triggers this off: a visit to the dentist, a job interview, your exams, having to get up and make a speech, asking someone out on a date, making a telephone call, going to the supermarket, etc, etc. It's quite amazing how your subconscious mind can panic at the slightest prospect of doing something that makes it feel uncomfortable.

This self-monitoring system that we all have in our lives can be very restricting and in many cases it completely dominates and controls our lives. This often leads to the inability even to attempt anything new and only serves to keep us well and truly stuck in the

Facing your fears enables you to burst out of the confines of your comfort zone and declare to yourself that you deserve a higher frequency life.

frequency zone that we are used to. This means we are stopping ourselves from moving forward in our lives and are constantly affirming to ourselves that we don't deserve love. In other words, the fact that we hold down our personal energy frequency at the lower levels says to us that we belong there and we don't belong at the higher frequency levels, where, of course, the energy that we call love exists. The repercussions of this are that our lives will be much more difficult, stuck at the lower frequency levels and attaining any real happiness within our lives will be extremely hard to achieve. Everything will be harder for us, relationships, work, leisure, you name it and it will be affected by our frequency level.

How many times have you seen somebody terrified of getting up and singing on a karaoke machine? Then once they have pushed themselves through this fear you cannot get the microphone out of their hands! They have faced a fear, which makes them feel elated, and it is also a major step forward in changing their programming. Facing your fears is a marvellous way of improving your life and it helps you to have more belief that you are deserving of the energy that we call love.

You need to identify your fears and draw up a plan of action so that you can tackle them one by one. This is a wonderful exercise and a very powerful statement to yourself that you deserve love. What actually happens when you face a fear is you go from very low-vibrational thoughts as you anticipate the coming challenge (self-doubt: 'I'm not good enough. What if I fail?') to very high-vibrational thoughts when you succeed ('I did it, I succeeded. I'm worthy.'). This means your energy field goes from low-vibrational to high-vibrational very quickly and it is a wonderful feeling of exhilaration.

What's the Bottom Line?

Our relationships struggle for one reason and one reason only: our insecurities. It is the negative thought patterns that we carry about ourselves that cause all our problems. The amount and intensity of our negative thought patterns determines how far our vibration rate will be below the vibration of love. Our innate and basic driving desire is to go home, which means to put our personal energy vibration back to the frequency of love where we belong.

Almost everything that we do in this life has hidden in it somewhere the desire to get high, feel better about ourselves or increase our vibration. This is why the beginning of a relationship is so wonderful; there is nothing like falling in love to boost our vibration. The good news is you don't have to lose that wonderful feeling, because with HVT you can at last have some control and learn how to keep your relationship in the high zone or, if you have slipped down to the mid zone, HVT can get you back up.

Think about it for a moment. If you were vibrating at the vibration of love, you would not need anything or anybody to make you feel good, and because you were there in your own right, nobody could take it away from you. You would spend your life in a state of total bliss and you would have found the secret to happiness. This is the journey that we call life, the journey back to the vibration of love.

Your Progress to Great Relationships

This section is designed to help you monitor your own progress over a six-week period, incorporating practical exercises to effect change. The aim of these exercises is to help you become more high-frequency in your general thinking process and to eliminate low-frequency thought patterns that you may have been carrying. This will have the effect of increasing your personal energy frequency, which in turn will push out the barriers of your comfort zone.

The programme for self-improvement that I am setting you is over a six-week period. In my experience, this is an optimum time period to initiate change, although I strongly recommend that you repeat this six-week work model four times, with a one-week rest week in between each of the six weeks. This will take you a total of twenty-seven weeks, which is the six months that I find cements permanent change.

I would like you to think carefully about your decision to accept that you are responsible for your life and put this in writing, as this will strengthen your belief. A form of acceptance of your responsibilities is given on page 118.

I would like you to dedicate your commitment to this six-week programme to somebody very special to you, and a form for this is also provided for you (see page 119). This will help you to stay focused when your subconscious begins to complain.

Each week you will read out to yourself six high-vibrational affirmations, each one to be read 10 times every morning and also in the evening. The first affirmation for each week is provided for you; you must create the other five as part of your task.

You are also required to do a visualisation exercise each day for the six-week period. This is to comfort your inner child and see yourself in a positive, high-vibrational situation. Try to find five minutes each morning to carry out this exercise and this will get your day off to a good start, as it will have the effect of dispersing any low-vibrational energy that may be pulling down your personal energy frequency. The first week's visualisation exercise has already been provided for you on page 105, but you will need to make up your own visualisation for the remaining five weeks. You can tailor this to your own personal requirements.

It is very important to plan your visualisation exercise carefully and write it into your timetable.

Use these pages to write your own affirmations, make notes on your personal visualisations and tick off when you have completed your tasks. It will help you to keep on track, give you focus and purpose, and also reassure you that things are improving all the time. Good Luck!

Accept responsibility for your life

Everybody needs to accept full responsibility for their life, as this is the first step to really changing our lives for the better and for good.

I would like you to write down the following acceptance statement, filling in your name, and read it out loud to yourself.

'I .... from this day forward accept full responsibility for my life and I realise that there is no

point in holding on to any low-vibrational feelings and emotions from the past. I release any negative energy that I am pointlessly holding on to and from this moment I accept total responsibility.'

Repeat this to yourself, as you see yourself letting go of all the low-vibrational energy and allow your energy frequency to rise as you move your life forward into a new and exciting future. You can read through your acceptance statement any time you feel your old low-vibrational feelings creeping back in.

Committed decision

The next step is to commit totally to the next six weeks and to be focused on your goal. We will work on six weeks because that is a comfortable time period to be able to stay determined and in control without too much interference from your subconscious mind.

To give added strength to your commitment, I would like you to dedicate the next six weeks to somebody very important to you and put the dedication in writing. It might be your son or daughter or your mother and father or perhaps in memory of a loved one: do it for them. This act of dedication will strengthen your will power and help sustain you in moments of weakness when your subconscious begins to complain.

I would like you to write the following and read it out loud to yourself:

'I .... commit to the next six weeks with all of the strength in my being and I am totally focused on my goal. I will succeed in my desire to carry out the exercises and disciplines required of me and I will not fail. I dedicate the following six weeks to .... and I will make you very proud of me.'

Anytime that you feel your will power begin to weaken you can refer back to your dedication to reinforce your commitment.

Week 1
My affirmations

▶ I love and approve of myself.

▶ . . . .

▶ . . . .

▶ . . . .

▶ . . . .

▶ . . . .

Comfort your inner child visualisation (see page 105)

My checklist

Day	Morning affirmations	Visualisation	Evening affirmations
Monday			
Tuesday			
Wednesday			
Thursday			
Friday			
Saturday			
Sunday			

Week 2
My affirmations

▸ I have a very positive, healthy relationship.

▸ ....

▸ ....

▸ ....

▸ ....

▸ ....

Comfort your inner child visualisation

My checklist

Day	Morning affirmations	Visualisation	Evening affirmations
Monday			
Tuesday			
Wednesday			
Thursday			
Friday			
Saturday			
Sunday			

Week 3
My affirmations

▸ I am vibrating in the high zone.

▸ . . . .

▸ . . . .

▸ . . . .

▸ . . . .

▸ . . . .

Comfort your inner child visualisation

My checklist

Day	Morning affirmations	Visualisation	Evening affirmations
Monday			
Tuesday			
Wednesday			
Thursday			
Friday			
Saturday			
Sunday			

Week 4
My affirmations

▶ I radiate powerful positive energy.

▶ ....

▶ ....

▶ ....

▶ ....

▶ ....

Comfort your inner child visualisation

My checklist

Day	Morning affirmations	Visualisation	Evening affirmations
Monday			
Tuesday			
Wednesday			
Thursday			
Friday			
Saturday			
Sunday			

Week 5
My affirmations

▶ My relationship is loving and high-vibrational.

▶ . . . .

▶ . . . .

▶ . . . .

▶ . . . .

▶ . . . .

Comfort your inner child visualisation

My checklist

Day	Morning affirmations	Visualisation	Evening affirmations
Monday			
Tuesday			
Wednesday			
Thursday			
Friday			
Saturday			
Sunday			

Week 6
My affirmations

▸ I have no insecurities about my relationship.

▸ . . . .

▸ . . . .

▸ . . . .

▸ . . . .

▸ . . . .

Comfort your inner child visualisation

My checklist

Day	Morning affirmations	Visualisation	Evening affirmations
Monday			
Tuesday			
Wednesday			
Thursday			
Friday			
Saturday			
Sunday			

Index